T0062886

Story of
Judah and Tamar

Birthright in Scripture

Joseph Ng Bak Soon

PARTRIDGE

Copyright © 2016 by Joseph Ng Bak Soon.

ISBN: Softcover   978-1-4828-5355-1
               eBook   978-1-4828-5356-8

All rights reserved. No part of this book may be used or reproduced by any means, graphic, electronic, or mechanical, including photocopying, recording, taping or by any information storage retrieval system without the written permission of the author except in the case of brief quotations embodied in critical articles and reviews.

Because of the dynamic nature of the Internet, any web addresses or links contained in this book may have changed since publication and may no longer be valid. The views expressed in this work are solely those of the author and do not necessarily reflect the views of the publisher, and the publisher hereby disclaims any responsibility for them.

ESV
Unless otherwise indicated, all scripture quotations are from The Holy Bible, English Standard Version® (ESV®). Copyright ©2007 update by Crossway Bibles, a division of Good News Publishers. Used by permission. All rights reserved.

Print information available on the last page.

To order additional copies of this book, contact
Toll Free 800 101 2657 (Singapore)
Toll Free 1 800 81 7340 (Malaysia)
orders.singapore@partridgepublishing.com

www.partridgepublishing.com/singapore

Contents

Acknowledgments

This book is dedicated to my family and friends who have been by my side through the good and sometimes not so good years, the years of "plenty" as well as the years of "famine." Through the tumble of life's ups and downs, joys and tears, you have all been there.

It is through this journey together—a very human journey—that God works out His divine purpose in each and every one of us, His children, regardless of the vagaries of life.

I also offer this work in prayer to all those who are about to read it:

May God guide each one of you, dear readers, uniquely according to His divine purpose and unerring hand, and so bless you in His abundance by bringing you into your divine "birthright" as He did Judah and Tamar so very long ago. Indeed it is a birthright prepared for you from the foundation of the earth.

—Joseph Ng

Story of Judah and Tamar

The Depths of God versus the Things of Man

Introduction

The story of Judah and Tamar in Genesis 38 is a familiar one in the Christian Bible. Nevertheless, it is also a dubious chapter in biblical scholarship because its narrative of the incestuous relationship between the patriarch Judah and his daughter-in-law seems out of place within the larger context of the life of Abraham, Isaac, Jacob and Joseph. In fact most commentaries on the Book of Genesis do not waste much ink on this chapter. There are prominent theologians who insist that this episode plays no role whatsoever in Genesis and that it should not even be inserted into the divine record.

The depths of God However, what is included by the Holy Spirit is not so easily dismissed by the doubts and cleverness of men. It is the contention of this author that the story of Judah and Tamar properly understood is integral to Genesis and the Scripture as a whole, and that its reverent interpretation enhances our appreciation of the Christian God. This is evidenced by the high regards given to themes arising from this seemingly insignificant pericope in both the Old and New Testament.

Rather than invoking skepticism, this brief but significant account in the Bible should alert Christians to a deep mystery in the divine revelation concerning God's identity, and His abiding relevance for present day Christian life, living and experience. The decision whether to leave Genesis 38 in or out of the divine record has a bearing on the integrity of the Scripture, and the experience of the people of God. While modern historical critical scholarship has its merits (within limits prescribed by its method); it is well to keep in mind that there is such a thing as the depths of God revealed through the Spirit versus the things of man however learned (1 Cor. 2:10).

The things of man Certainly few today would claim that Genesis 38 has a pivotal position in the Book of Genesis, much less the rest of Christian Scripture. Many modern scholars view this story with its sexually explicit and apparently secular narratives as an anomaly. Westermann, for instance, recognized the purpose of the story as being for "the greater good" and "protecting the community."[1]

The attribution of this motif is commendable, but the failure to see a divine purpose at work is to miss the blessing that is implicit in this story. In his monumental three-volume work on Genesis, he rightfully asserted that "the narrative of Judah and Tamar has not been inserted into the Joseph story; it has nothing to do with it, but rather is an insertion into the Jacob story, into its conclusion

---

1. C. Westermann, *Genesis 37–50: A Continental Commentary* (Minneapolis: Fortress, 2002), 56–57.

(the traditional material of Genesis 37 and chapters 46 to 50)."[2] According to this view, the explanation of the meaning of Genesis 38 should be situated within the wider canvas of the story of Jacob, coinciding with Jacob's maturing years (37–50),[3] and not within that of his son, Joseph.

Overall, however, Westermann is less than convinced about the cohesion of its parts and theological significance. He is of the opinion that verses 1 to 11, the introductory material to the story of Judah and Tamar, is relatively independent of verses 27 to 30, which close the story with the birth of Perez and Zerah—the twin sons of Judah with his daughter-in-law, Tamar. He reasoned that both parts provide details that are not necessary for the narrative in verses 12 to 26. These verses slow down the account to the bold action Tamar took to beget offspring with her father-in-law (Judah)—for her deceased husband, Er, Judah's eldest son. In this way, the composition thus overloads the function of the exposition and the conclusion.[4] In Westermann's opinion, Genesis 38 is "a secular narrative through and through ... The narrative is secular and says nothing of God's action or speech, and that theology is not necessary for an understanding of the narration."[5]

Gerhard Von Rad is no less skeptical of the unity of chapter 38 within the patriarchal narratives. He sees the story of Judah and

---

2. Ibid., 37–50, 49.

3. See Appendix G: "Time Extent of Genesis 38", for a graphical depiction of the story of Judah and Tamar, mapped against that of the three stages of Jacob's life.

4. C. Westermann, *Genesis 37–50*, 49.

5. Ibid., 56–57.

Tamar as an insertion by the Yahwist (a postulated early source that is supposed to have provided a strand of the narrative in the five books of Moses), whose decision it was to place the account here in recognition of the succession of tradition among the Israelites, but that it has no connection at all to the strictly organized Joseph story. He treats this passage as a completely independent unit, standing almost on its own. "This compact narrative requires for its interpretation none of the other Patriarchal narratives ..."[6]

However, Von Rad acceded to the possibility of constructing a theology of this passage[7] in that he says, "The theological substance of this story can only derive from the material character of the saving gifts toward which Israel's ancestors directed their life." He further commented, "In contrast to the majority of Abraham and Jacob narratives, this story is not concerned with the Promised Land, but with the blessing of great progeny." These two comments by Von Rad are conducive in part to the literary and theological unity of the story of Judah and Tamar in Genesis; yet, I wonder about the appropriateness of Von Rad's opinion regarding the absolute independence of this unit—that it requires no other part of the patriarchal narratives for its interpretation.

A word on approach The thesis advanced in this book is that the key to unveil the story in Genesis 38 is located in the concept of a believers' birthright. The word "birthright" appears six times in the Book of Genesis (Gen. 25:31, 32, 33, 34; 27:36;

---

6. G. Von Rad, *Genesis: A Commentary by Gerhard Von Rad.* 2nd ed. (Philadelphia: The Westminster Press, 1972), 356–357.

7. Ibid., 362.

43:33), five of which referenced the incident on its transfer from Esau to Jacob in Genesis 25. There we see the firstborn of Isaac, Esau selling his birthright to his younger brother Jacob for a bowl of stew (25:29–34). When we encounter this story as a modern reader, we may not realize the criticality of the birthright in Scripture. Yet, this event is of such monumental importance that the New Testament writer of the Epistle to the Hebrews warned against falling away from the grace of God through the profanity of Esau who for one meal gave up his birthright (Heb. 12:15–16).

The volume you hold in your hand will give you a good appreciation of the importance of a Christian's birthright from the story of Judah and Tamar specifically; and also how this concept operates at a deep level in Genesis and the rest of Scripture. An understanding of what the birthright is and how it relates to our participation in God's promise is crucial to opening up the Christian Bible to our experience. The seemingly obscure role of the event in Genesis 38 has been noted by many biblical scholars. It is the conviction of this author that without some appreciation of the significance of the birthright in Scripture, we would miss the full import of the relevance of the story of Judah and Tamar in the patriarchal narrative in Genesis.

Hence, given that this story is a disputed one in Genesis, we will proceed carefully and in detail along five lines of inquiry to cut straight the word of the truth:

Part 1. Examine the literary role and function of the story of Judah and Tamar in Genesis. Here, we query the text for clues to the textual intention of Genesis 38 within the patriarchal narrative and Scripture as a whole,

Part 2. Interpret the meaning of this story in historical context within the deep literary structure of the life of the patriarchs, informed by a key concept embedded in Genesis—participation in birthright. What is advocated is a reading that respect the first Testament in its own historical integrity,

Part 3. Survey a biblical approach that vests interpretive authority in the final form of Christian Scripture as received by the church—the canon of Scripture. Armed with the "rule of faith," the accepted canon gives Christians a present insight into the first Testament that is authoritative in that it is in concord with the hermeneutics of Jesus and the apostles,

Part 4. Apply an ecumenical "rule of faith" of the church fathers to birthright in a two-testament Scripture that sees the event in Genesis 38 as embryonic—as it is God's action in the *pre-incarnated* Christ for the realization of kingship as God's eternal intention for mankind. The significance of birthright as manifested in the dynamics of God's ordination and individual responsibility in the story of Judah and Tamar is realized as grace and responsibility in the kingdom in the *incarnated* Christ in the New Testament, and

Part 5. Draw out the relevance and application of the story of Judah and Tamar within the context of a believer's salvation for reigning in Christ's life in the church as the body of Christ today.

That which has been written in the word of God is meant for all, for God Himself desires all men to be saved and to come to the full knowledge of the truth (1 Tim. 2:4). When the disciples wanted to know who is the greatest in the kingdom of heaven (Matt. 18:1), Jesus called a child to Him—and by way of emphasis—put the child in their midst. Then Jesus answered them, "... Truly, I say to you, unless you turn and become like children, you will never enter the kingdom of heaven. Whoever humbles himself like this child is the greatest in the kingdom of heaven" (vv. 3–4). The things of the kingdom of God are meant for little children for it is a matter of the life of God (John 3:3, 5). Every human child can understand the things of man; even so every child of God can apprehend the things of God.

In this respect, it is the unfortunate tendency for many works of Christian scholarship to be verbose, opaque and inaccessible to a general audience. Much effort has been expended in this volume to ensure that what is contained here does justice to God's intention for every child of God.

Yet, the truth is two sided.

The apostle Paul admonished a young Timothy to be "... diligent to present yourself approved to God as a workman who does not need to be ashamed, accurately handling the word of truth" (2 Tim. 2:15, NASB).

It is my hope for you as a child of God that your diligence in entering into the discussion in this volume will be richly rewarded in Him who is able to do superabundantly above all that we ask or think (Eph. 3:20).

Part 1: Setting the Story

Overview

Part 1 begins by noting the abiding influence of Westermann and Von Rad on the interpretation of the story of Judah and Tamar in contemporary scholarship. While benefiting from their contributions, we also direct attention to what is left unanswered by their inquiries. A possible way forward is alluded to by B. K Waltke who recognized Genesis 38 as answering who among the sons of Jacob would have the right of the firstborn. The right of the firstborn is very much related to God's eternal intention for mankind. So the story of Judah and Tamar must be understood from within the textual setting of God's recovery of that intention through the promise given to Abraham and his descendants.

Section Outline

Part 1: Setting the Story

Section Introduction

1. Why this story?
- o A promising way forward

2. God's intention for mankind
- o God's intent and the tree of life
- o The toledot formula and God's recovery of fallen mankind

3. Narrative context: the life of Jacob and Joseph
- o The main plot is Jacob's life
- o The subplot belongs to Joseph, Judah and Tamar

4. Scriptural context: God's promise to Abraham
- o Transmission of the promise
- o Preeminence of Abraham, Isaac and Jacob

5. The God of Abraham, Isaac and Jacob
- o God's Triune identity
- o Entering into the promise of Abraham, Isaac and Jacob

Section Summary

Setting the Story

Section Introduction

Westermann and Von Rad's influence are still evident in contemporary works on Genesis. Allen P. Ross, in his *Creation and Blessing: A Guide to the Study of Genesis,*[1] echoes Westermann: "This chapter has been dubbed a secular story because it does not have a great emphasis on God's acting or speaking in the events." Even though Ross admits to God's providential protection of the community, he has this limiting view of the theological scope of Genesis 38: "The closest that we come to a theological point is Judah's statement that Tamar had been more righteous than he" (v. 26).[2]

Even a personage as eminent as the Lutheran Old Testament scholar on liturgics H. C. Leupold, in his commentary on Genesis, sees little use for this chapter in Christian preaching.

---

1. A. P. Ross, *Creation and Blessing: A Guide to the Study of Genesis* (Grand Rapids, MI: Baker, 1998), 612–613.

2. See Part 3: Back to the Present, for an alternate assessment to the theological reach and scope of Genesis 38 in view of a two-testament Christian Scripture.

He dismissed it as "entirely unsuited to homiletical use, much as the devout Bible student may glean from the chapter."[3] One cannot help but wonder why it has this dubious reputation. Aside from its coverage of matters not generally mentioned in polite society: sexual intercourse, coitus interruptus (because one of the character in the story, Onan spilled his seed on the ground deliberately), and prostitution; perhaps the curious location of Genesis 38 may have something to do with this. This chapter, sandwiched between the story of Joseph's sale to Egypt in chapter 37 and his slavery in chapter 39, seems to continue seamlessly without the intervening story of Judah and Tamar.

1. Why this story?

The question arises as to why this story is in the Bible at all? More recent evangelical scholarship generally claims it highlights the need for continuity of the promised seed through the line of Judah. In the process, the contextual narrative brings out the dysfunctional nature of Jacob's family (chapter 37), Judah's faithlessness, and Tamar's scheme (chapter 38). Add to these God's sovereignty and the situation is turned. Catastrophe is averted, and the line of the promised seed continues with Judah's son Pharez, leading to King David and finally the Messiah.[4]

---

3. H. C. Leupold, *Genesis II* (Grand Rapids: Baker, 1942), 990.

4. See B. K. Waltke, *Genesis: A Commentary*; J. H. Sailhamer, *The Pentateuch as Narrative*; A. P. Ross, *Creation & Blessing: A Guide to the Study and Exposition of Genesis*; and S. Greidanus, *Preaching Christ from Genesis: Foundations for Expository Sermons* for typical expositions of this nature.

While this reading is scriptural, it does not counter Von Rad's conviction that Genesis 38 is an independent unit that doesn't require the other patriarchal narratives for its interpretation. Von Rad also regards this chapter as having no connection with the tightly organized Joseph story. This approach also leaves Westermann's comment on the lack of cohesion in the chapter largely unanswered.

It is the purpose of this book to show that the cohesion of Genesis 38 must be demonstrated from within the deep structure of the story of Abraham, Isaac, and Jacob—not just from the oft-quoted verse for great progeny in Genesis 3:15. There is no denying that chapter 38 preserves the continuity of Judah's line, from which the "seed of woman" would eventually come. But in lieu of Westermann and Von Rad's objections,[5] such an approach, while doctrinally correct, doesn't answer the question of intratextual cohesion within the story of Judah and Tamar, and intertextual integrity of this unit when read alongside the patriarchal narratives, and the rest of Scripture.

A promising way forward   Among more recent works, that of Waltke's explicitly recognizes the role of Genesis 38 in addressing who among the twelve sons of Jacob had the right of the firstborn.[6] Building on this hint, a key dynamic in patriarchal narratives must

---

5. Westermann and Von Rad's objection raised the question of the absence of deep connection between the narratives of the lives of the patriarchs and the seeming insertion of the story of Judah and Tamar. I'm convinced this connection can be seen in the telling of the promises given to Abraham and his progeny, Isaac and Jacob, through a key operative concept in Genesis, that of the birthright.

6. B. K. Waltke, *Genesis: A Commentary*, 492. This is influenced by a study conducted by Goldin, "The Youngest Son."

be brought to the forefront. A major theme of this book is that the cohesion and integrity of the story of Judah and Tamar are found in the transmission of the promise given to Abraham in his calling in Genesis 12. The dynamics of this transmission, based on the right of the firstborn, provides the glue that preserves the organic integrity of Genesis 38. When this process is made more explicit, Judah and Tamar's story is seen as pivotal within the wider context of the story of Abraham, Isaac and Jacob.

2. God's intention for mankind

Old Testament scholarship recognizes that the literary structure of Genesis is built around ten occurrences of "generations," or the Hebrew *toledot*. From a structural perspective, the toledot formula provides a natural schema for recounting God's untiring effort to return fallen humanity to the original intention of His creation described in Genesis 1 and 2. God's intention is that an individual, in His image and likeness and the apex of His creative activity, be committed with God's authority and dominion, so the person may rule and reign as God's regent on earth (Gen. 1:26–28).

God's intent and the tree of life The God-ordained way to fulfill one's destiny is through the Tree of Life, a tree in the Garden of Eden, representing God[7] as the source of human

---

7. God is life in His Trinitarian being. The Father is life (John 5:26), the Son is life (John 14:6), and the Spirit is the Spirit of life (Rom. 8:2). Moreover, the incarnation of the Son is so that we may have an abundant life (John 10:10; Col. 2:2; 3:4). As such, the tree of life is not only in Genesis 2 and Revelation 21 and 22. It also appears in the symbol of the true vine, the cultivated vine in John 15, with the Father as the husbandmen, the Son as the vine tree, and the believers as the branches abiding in the vine. The Father is the source of life, and the Son is the embodiment of the Father as life.

life (Gen. 2:8–9, 17). This subject in itself is worthy of a book length exposition, but suffice here to mention that God's life is the key to His dominion and kingdom for humankind. A particular kingdom is the totality of a certain kind of life. The animal kingdom for instance is the totality of the animal life. By the same token, God's kingdom is the manifestation and totality of God's life and the activities of His life. In this regards, the developing light of later Scripture says unless one is born again, that is, born of water (baptism) and the Spirit (born anew)—hence born of God—he or she cannot see, much less enter the kingdom of God (John 1:13; 3:3, 5–6). The implication is that God's kingdom is the realm of God's life, and rebirth is the only entrance possible.

In this sense, the significance of the fall in Genesis 3 was that created Adam (together with Eve) rejected this God-ordained way. Instead they opted for a way independent of God's life, that is, the way of the Tree of Knowledge of Good and Evil (Gen. 2:9b, 17; 3:2–7), a way of absolute self-determination, and by implication, absolute autonomy and independence from God. This resulted in humanity's existence and living outside the realm of God's life.

Humanity's condition outside the Garden of Eden (3:23–24) is one that is contrary to the divine intention God has for Adam and Eve. Our forbear may have failed in the garden, but God is NOT in the business of giving up on mankind. From the vantage point of His eternal intent, the excursus taken by humankind since the Fall is temporal. God's plan is the issue of His determined counsel (Eph. 1:10). It changes not from generation to generation. The Scripture beginning with Genesis is the record of the determined counsel of His will as manifested in the history of the human race, and so embedded in Genesis is the seed plot of a divine program for mankind's recovery back to His original intention.

The toledot formula and God's recovery of fallen mankind In the Book of Genesis, the first toledot (Hebrew word for "account" or "generation" in Gen. 2:4) serves as a summary statement to God's completed creation. The other nine occurrences (5:1; 6:9; 10:1; 11:10; 11:27; 25:12; 25:19; 36:1; 37:2) reveal how God works untiringly from generation to generation—Adam, Noah and Noah's sons, Shem, Terah, Ishmael, Isaac, Esau, and Jacob—in a cosmic recovery effort to avert the effect of humanity's fall.

I venture that in the final analysis, the heart of the all-loving God is such that the teleology (end goal) of His saving effort includes the lines of Ishmael and Esau, along with the rest of humankind. After all, His clear promise to Abraham was that through Him (the unique seed of Abraham), all the families of the earth would be blessed (12:3b; 28:14). Due to human biases and discriminations, it is easy to forget that God has a universal program that includes all of humankind. Indeed, from the beginning, God's heart is towards all of humanity, regardless of race, creed and culture. As the apostle Paul expresses it, "God our Savior ... desires all man to be saved and to come to the full knowledge of the truth" (1 Tim. 2:3–4).

Genesis Chapters 3 to 11 portray the descending pattern of man's departure from God's intent. After humanity's rebellion and rejection reached a climax at the Tower of Babel (Gen. 11), the focus of God's activity turned to the line of Abraham, son of Terah (v. 27). Through this line, God's salvation work operated through the generations of Abraham's descendants as proxy for the rest of fallen humankind. The promise of the seed of woman in Genesis 3:15 is the crux of this salvation plan, and seen in the light of the New Testament, God's promise to Abraham in Genesis 12:1–3 is the beginning of the development of this motif (Gal. 3:17–19, 22, 29). In the truest sense, Abraham inherited the promise of God for the rest of humankind! That blessing which culminates in the salvation of the world (John 3:16) would first be handed down to his son Isaac, and then Jacob in the following generations. From this point forward, three names become important in Genesis: Abraham, Isaac, and Jacob.

3. Narrative context: the life of Jacob and Joseph

The immediate context for the story of Judah and Tamar is the betrayal of Jacob's favorite eleventh son, Joseph at the hands of his brothers. Joseph's betrayal falls within the tenth and final toledot in the account or generation of Jacob's descendants (starting with Gen. 37:2). This section coincides with Jacob's maturing years (Gen. 37–50)—the final stage of his long pilgrimage with the God of his fathers. The life of Jacob can be summarized in three stages: His years of striving (25–31), his breaking (32–36), and his maturing years (37–50). If we believe in the Scripture as God's word, such a record cannot be coincidental, for the apostle Paul himself had written concerning the events in the Old

Testament to the Corinthians, "Now these things happened to them as an example, but they were written down for our instruction, on whom the end of the ages has come" (1 Cor. 10:11).

The main plot is Jacob's life In Genesis, the controlling stories of Jacob's life spans an impressive twenty-six chapters (25–50), an account more than half of the entire length of fifty chapters. If the author of Genesis sees it fit to devote that much narrative space to Jacob, we should know that it deserves much attention. The record concerning Jacob's beloved son, Joseph is nested within this larger section (37–50).[8] Judah and Tamar's story is just a single chapter (Gen. 38), immediately following the account of Joseph's sale to the Ishmaelites in chapter 37. There we see Joseph's fate bound tragically for slavery in Egypt, but God in His sovereignty has the last word on this, so He may bring some good out of evil (50:20).

The subplot belongs to Joseph, Judah and Tamar From a structural perspective, Westermann and Von Rad both concur that the story of Judah and Tamar should be seen as an insertion into Jacob's story rather than that of Joseph's. The implication is that, although the immediate context for analysis of Genesis 38 is Joseph's life, the operating dynamics in the story of Judah and Tamar are found within the wider concerns of Jacob's life. The narrative of Jacob's life is of particular significance in Genesis.

---

8. As Westermann observed, the story of Judah and Tamar also falls within this larger pericope of Jacob's maturing years.

This is borne out in the construction of the text of Genesis, which focuses on Jacob and the circumstances that touches his life. Even when Jacob's name recedes, as in portions of Joseph's story, the incidents and events narrated pertain to God's dealings with Jacob in order that he may have the reality of his God-given namesake, Israel (Gen. 35:10). The Hebrew name Israel, or "God prevails" is a fitting epitaph to Jacob's experience of the God of his fathers, for throughout his life God struggled with him, and in the end Jacob overcame what he was by nature to become who God wants him to be.

In this way, God's sovereignty in executing His promise to Abraham is exercised over every incident and event in Jacob's life from Genesis 25 to 50. Jacob's eventual maturity in life allows him to become worthy of his name in the roll call of God as the God of Abraham, Isaac, and Jacob,[9] in spite of his rather poor beginning. The narrative of Judah and Tamar is as it were, a lesser but nevertheless prominent scene painted on the larger canvas of God's pivotal work on Jacob. In this sense Genesis 38, though occupying a single chapter in Jacob's life, plays a key role in God's fulfillment of His promise to Abraham.

---

9. N. Watchman, *The Collected Works of Watchman Nee: The God of Abraham, Isaac, and Jacob*, set two, vol. 35 (Anaheim, CA: LSM, 1993). As will be seen later, Nee's insight on the God of Abraham, Isaac, and Jacob is useful in highlighting the canonical focus of God's work of grace upon these three men.

4. Scriptural context: God's promise to Abraham

The canonical context (a theological perspective from Scripture) for Genesis 38 should be situated within God's specific work on the three men Abraham, Isaac, and Jacob in relation to the transmission of God's promise. When God called Abraham, He asked him to leave his country, his kindred, and his father's house for a land that He would show him (Gen. 12:1). God also promised Abraham that he would make him a great nation and that he would be a blessing to the nations (v. 2).

Transmission of the promise This promise was later handed down to Isaac, Abraham's only son through Sarah. God told Isaac, "I am the God of Abraham your father. Fear not, for I am with you and will bless you and multiply your offspring for my servant Abraham's sake" (Gen. 26:24).

From Isaac the promise went to Jacob.

God said to Jacob, "I am the Lord, the God of Abraham your father, and the God of Isaac. The land on which you lie I will give to you and to your offspring. Your offspring shall be like the dust of the earth, and you shall spread abroad to the west and to the east and to the north and to the south, and in you and your offspring shall all the families of the earth be blessed" (28:13–14).

Four centuries later, God would pick up this strain again and tell the Israelites, "I will bring you into the land that I swore to give to Abraham, to Isaac, and to Jacob. I will give it to you for a possession. I am the Lord." (Exod. 6:8). These passages show that the Israelites as a nation entered into the inheritance of three very specific men. In a sense the Israelites did not have an inheritance of their own. And to enter into the inheritance of these three men was to be ushered into a particular relationship— experiencing the work of God that would make them the people of God. Not any God, but specifically the God of Abraham, Isaac, and Jacob.

Preeminence of Abraham, Isaac and Jacob The canon of Scripture testifies to the preeminence of God's attention on these three men. The significance of this can be seen throughout the Scripture. The God who called Abraham out is the God of Abraham, Isaac, and Jacob. In Exodus 3:6, God revealed His identity to Moses, "I am the God of your father, the God of Abraham, the God of Isaac, and the God of Jacob." God said this in the Old Testament. In the New Testament the Lord Jesus similarly affirmed, again emphasizing whose God He is. "I am the God of Abraham and the God of Isaac and the God of Jacob" is quoted in all the Synoptics (Matt. 22:32, Mark 12:26, and Luke 20:37). We are also told that we would see "Abraham and Isaac and Jacob … in the kingdom of God" (Luke 13:28), and that "many will come from east and west and will recline at the table with Abraham, Isaac, and Jacob in the kingdom of the heaven" (Matt. 8:11).

5. The God of Abraham, Isaac and Jacob

And so with remarkable consistency throughout both Testaments, God bears witness to the special grace He extended to Abraham, Isaac, and Jacob; whose experiences with Him would eventually find fulfillment in the pattern of God's saving work on mankind as Father, Son, and Holy Spirit. Our God is the God of Abraham, Isaac, and Jacob (Exo. 3:16). This revelation would in time be fulfilled in a great name that was to break forth on the earth through God's incarnation in the Son—in the singular name of the unique God of all Christians with the plural labels of Father, Son and Holy Spirit: "Go therefore and make disciples of all nations, baptizing them in the name [singular] of the Father and of the Son and of the Holy Spirit" (Matt. 28:19).

God's Triune identity These observations from Scripture hint that God's dealings with Abraham, Isaac, and Jacob reflect the imprint of His Triune identity; and so God's work on these three men would be representative of His saving work on future descendants of Abraham—not just the Israelites but all those who are of faith in Christ Jesus (Gal. 3:16, 18, 22, 26).

Thus, in effecting a salvation that would operate through the millennia, God first began a specific work of grace on these three men as a collective unit, reflective of His identity as Father, Son, and Holy Spirit. The canonical or biblical testimony from both the Old and New Testament is that to enter into the inheritance of these three men is a very special thing indeed, for it is to enter into a very specific blessing, relationship, and work of God that would find eventual consummation in His recovery of all things, according to His heart's intent.

Entering into the promise of Abraham, Isaac and Jacob It was for this purpose that God became the God of these three specific men, that they would have certain experiences with Him that would constitute them as the people of God. And in inheriting these promises, the children of Israel would enter into a covenant relationship with the God of their fathers, and so ushered into the same work of grace collectively as a nation—a work that would make them the people of God, a special treasure to Him above all others (Exod. 19:3–6). In this way God intends to show His kindness, not only to the Israelites but, in the fullness of time, also to all nations of the earth.

Given the emphasis of God's work on these men in Genesis, even Joseph's life and that of Judah and Tamar must of necessity be seen as part of God's dealings with Jacob, and not independent of it.

Henceforth, the God of Genesis would be known specifically as the God of Abraham, Isaac, and Jacob. So it is not enough for the people of God to just claim or reclaim Abraham. They must be able to proclaim by experience that their God is the God of Abraham, Isaac, and Jacob. The people of God are those who have entered into the same work of grace as that of these men.

They are those who can trace their definitive spiritual lineage to Abraham, Isaac, and Jacob.[10]

The grace of the God of Abraham, Isaac and Jacob is such that eventually, even the recalcitrant Judah, one of the two main characters of the subject of this book would be added to the roll call of God as the God of Abraham, Isaac and Jacob.

At the fullness of time, the New Testament would resound with these words: "The book of the genealogy of Jesus Christ … the Son of Abraham: Abraham was the father of Isaac, and Isaac the father of Jacob, and Jacob the father of Judah and his brothers … Now the birth of Jesus Christ took place in this way …" (Matt. 1:1–2, 18). We can see from here that Judah, a principle character in Genesis 38, is in the direct line of transmission of God's promise to Abraham, to Isaac, to Jacob, and then to Judah and his brothers … and finally to Jesus Christ!

Section summary   The story of Judah and Tamar in chapter 38 of Genesis has been controversial in the history of biblical interpretation. Its position and organic unity in the patriarchal narratives is not obvious, given that Genesis 39 on Joseph's slavery in Egypt can continue seamlessly from the end of chapter 37—on the sale of Joseph to the Ishmaelites—without the intervening account in chapter 38. It is generally agreed among contemporary evangelical scholars that the signal event for

---

10. The good news is that the New Testament has an inclusion clause, for they who are of faith in Christ Jesus are sons of Abraham (Gal. 3:7). In this sense all New Testament believers of Christ are included in this roll call of the God of Abraham, Isaac, and Jacob.

continuity is the promised seed of the woman (Gen. 3:15) through the line of Judah.

But the towering shadows of Westermann and Von Rad highlight the need to establish a deep organic association between Genesis 38 and the rest of the patriarchal narratives. The contention of this book is that the connection is to be found in the dynamics of the transmission of God's promise from Abraham to his progeny through their participation in this blessing according to the right of the firstborn.

It is the conviction of this author that a demonstration of this association requires both a literary and canonical approach.[11] Structurally, the story of Judah and Tamar is within the tenth toledot on the descendants of Jacob. The overarching span of Jacob's life from Genesis 25 to 50 is the context within which the account of Joseph, Judah, and Tamar finds its significance.

From the perspective of the New Testament, the name of Judah in the direct line of the descendants of Jesus—as it immediately follows that of Abraham, Isaac, and Jacob (Matt. 1:1–2)—hints of a key role for Genesis 38 in the transmission of God's promise given to Abraham. The significance of this observation is that although the story of Judah and Tamar is within the Joseph

---

11. *Part 2: Backtrack Four Thousand Years* emphasized a literary interpretive approach. *Part 3: Back to the Present* explores the implication of a canonical approach and the theology of Genesis 38 in view of the concept of the birthright, the right of the firstborn, in the story of Judah and Tamar.

pericope, its meaning and interpretation derives from the wider context of God's dealings with Abraham, Isaac and Jacob; particularly that of Jacob, given the prominence of his life in Genesis.

Part 2: Backtrack Four Thousand Years

Overview

Part 2 embarks on a quest to uncover relevant narrative strands on birthright in Genesis. We will dive into the text of Genesis 38 in particular (intratextual reading), though informed by other passages in Scripture (intertextual dynamics). A brief investigation of the historical circumstances surrounding the events recorded in the story will furnish other clues. The search is for an appropriate delineation of birthright in Genesis. Indeed, what is the birthright? Where is its first mention? What could possibly be its significance in the divine record? What we reap from our readings will give us an appreciation of the primacy of the birthright to the ancient—and it serves to reorient our understanding as to why the story of Judah and Tamar has to be where it is in Scripture.

Section Outline

Part 2: Backtrack Four Thousand Years

Section Introduction

6. The story of Judah and Tamar in historical context
- o Opening scene: Judah's falling away from his brothers
- o Levirate marriage: Preserving the line of Judah
- o Enters Tamar: A woman in God's plan
- o Tamar's scheme: A valiant struggle for the birthright
- o Judah's repentance: A successful turnaround—birthright regained

7. Blessing of Abraham and the transmission of the birthright
- o Birthright: God's sovereignty and man's responsibility
- o God initiates but man must respond
- o Principle of transferability

8. The constitution of the birthright
- o The land
- o The kingship
- o The priesthood

9. A quandary in Jacob's line
- o Esau disqualified
- o Reuben defiled
- o Simeon and Levi cursed

10. Where did the birthright go?
- o The birthright in the wider story of Jacob

11. Birthright: Key to the story of Judah and Tamar
- o Connecting Joseph to Judah
- o Qualifying Judah for the kingship
- o Pivotal position of Genesis 38

Section Summary

Backtrack

Four Thousand Years

Section Introduction

Our interpretation of the story of Judah and Tamar will involve travelling back four thousand years into the past. The events portrayed in Genesis 38 transpired in patriarchal times, circa second millennium BC. Given the gulf of time separating us, it is prudent that any effort to unravel its significance acquaint itself with some of the ethos of the time: the differing ethical mores, cultural values, and practices of the ancients that may have some bearing on this story. One of these as we will see is the levirate marriage, which hints of a key dynamic at play in this unit—that of the birthright, the right of the firstborn.

The dynamics of the birthright are embedded in the deep structure of the patriarchal narratives concerning the transmission of God's promise to Abraham, to Isaac, to Jacob, and eventually to Jacob's sons. In our development of this theme, we will focus particularly on the life of Jacob for reasons already identified in Part 1—that the pericope for analysis of Judah and Tamar's story be situated within the context of Jacob's life. In the process of tracing the transmission of the birthright from Isaac to Jacob, and then to Jacob's sons, the pivotal role of Genesis 38 will emerge from our reading.

6. The story of Judah and Tamar in historical context

The story of Judah and Tamar in Genesis 38 can be divided into two major sections: verses 1 to 11 and 12 to 30. The first section focuses on giving an account of Judah. Verse 1 tells of Judah departing from his brothers to visit his gentile friend Hirah, an Adullamite (v. 1), a resident of the village of Adullam.

The village of Adullam has been identified archaeologically with Tell esh Sheikh Madhkur, northwest of Hebron, at a lower elevation of 3,040 feet above sea level.[1] Ancient Adullam was a Canaanite city that controlled one of the passes into the hill country of Judah. It is first mentioned here in Genesis 38. By the time of Joshua 15:35, Adullam was mentioned as a royal city. There was a cave nearby called the cave of Adullam to which David and his followers fled for refuge from King Saul, after David was anointed by Samuel to replace Saul as king (1 Samuel 22:1).

---

1. J. H. Walton, V. H. Matthews, and M. W. Chavalas, *The IVP Background Commentary: Old Testament* (Downers Grove: IVP, 2000), 69–70.

Opening scene: Judah's falling away from his brothers When Judah departed from his brothers and turned aside to Hirah, the Adullamite, he was going away from his family to live among the Canaanites. The literal phrase in Hebrew for departing is "went down," (Gen. 38:1) and it is quite appropriate to describe Judah's journeying as "going down" from his brothers. He was after all descending geographically from Hebron to Adullam. In the preceding chapter, Judah had been complicit in proposing the sale of his younger brother Joseph to the Ishmaelites (37:26-27). When seen in light of this immediate act of betrayal, Judah's going down from Hebron to Adullam may also be symbolic. It speaks perhaps of Judah's falling away from his brothers, thus alluding to Judah's sense of failure and disappointment with himself in what he had done.

From the beginning of the patriarchal narrative, fraternity with gentiles was not encouraged. When Abraham wanted to find a wife for his son Isaac, he made his servant swear that he would not "take a wife for my son from the daughters of the Canaanites, among whom I dwell ..." (24:3). Consequently, Abraham's servant had to travel back a long way to his master's home city of Nahor in Mesopotamia (v. 10) to find a wife for Isaac from among Abraham's kindred (v. 4). So it stands to reason that Judah's long-term friendship with Hiram, his marriage to a Canaanite woman (38:2), and his settling down in Adullam for over twenty years[2] to

---

2. G. Sidney, *Preaching Christ from Genesis: Foundations for Expository Sermons* (Grand Rapids: Eerdmans, 2007), 360.

raise a family away from his brothers, hints strongly of a sense of shame and despair[3] over his personal failings.

With this somewhat discouraging background as introduction to Judah's circumstances, the narration passes on swiftly to the wickedness and acts of his two older sons, Er and Onan. Judah's youngest, Selah would also have a role in this story, albeit a passive one (vv. 3-5).

Er was Judah's firstborn.

As was the practice at that time, Judah took a wife for his eldest son, Er. Her name was Tamar (v. 6). The biblical account is relatively silent on Tamar's life before she married into the family of Judah. But going by available evidence surrounding her name in Scripture, she was most likely a Canaanite. Without further ado, the narrator picks up his pace, and goes on to inform us that Er was slain by God because of his wickedness (v. 7).

---

3. Some commentators have an overtly dark portrayal of Judah. Take, for instance, John Phillips in his *Exploring Genesis: An Expository Commentary* (Grand Rapids: Kregel, 1980), 29. His perception of Judah can be seen in his choice of words: perverted values, personal vileness, pretended virtue. I will grant that within limits the more vile Judah is portrayed, the more God's grace will be seen to be magnified. Yes, Judah's condition is by no means satisfactory. But painting his vileness beyond what Scripture is willing to state risks giving the impression that God is willy-nilly in His selection of vessels for His plan. Although God has His prerogative, He is also not whimsical or arbitrary in His action. He is a God who sees into man's hearts and weighs it. As such it is more fitting to see Judah's condition as one of disappointment over his failures. Otherwise, what is the difference between Judah and his own wicked sons? God is not a respecter of persons in that He should excuse one and approve the other based on a whim. I believe that the all-seeing God has weighed Judah's heart and finds him capable of something nobler, even more than what he himself might suspect. God's selection is based first on His sovereignty and prerogative, but it also takes into account what is in man's heart, which only He knows accurately. Surely Judah's eventual turnaround justifies God's selection of him. In his return to his brothers, Judah would become critical to the reconciliation of Jacob's house.

Levirate Marriage: Preserving the line of Judah   According to an ancient custom, that of levirate marriage, Onan as the second born was obligated to raise up offspring to his brother with Tamar (v. 8), but he was negligent in this family responsibility due to selfishness. Whenever he cohabitated with Tamar, he deliberately "spilled his seed on the ground" (v. 9). For this direct dereliction of his duty as brother-in-law, God slew him also (v. 10).

Levirate marriage (brother-in-law marriage) was an ancient custom of the Israelites. It provided for the surviving brother to beget children from his sister-in-law, the firstborn of whom was regarded as the child of the deceased. Its first mention here in Scripture (38:8–10)[4] is direct evidence that the right of the firstborn is at work in this passage.

The meaning of levirate marriage as given in Deuteronomy is "the first son [firstborn son] whom she bears shall succeed to the name of his dead brother, that his name may not be blotted out of Israel" (Deut. 25:6). This is the primary purpose for the custom. All others were derived and therefore secondary. As Westermann rightly noted in relation to this verse in Deuteronomy, "It is only a secondary purpose of the levirate that the property of the deceased passes on to the one who is heir to his name, and is probably a later accretion."[5]

---

4. The levirate custom is found three times in the Old Testament: Gen 38, Deut. 25:5–10, and Ruth 4.

5. C. Westermann, *Genesis 37–50*, 52.

Later Israelite tradition (Deut. 25 and Ruth 4) provides for the levir (the brother who was to marry his sister-in-law) to refuse his obligation but through a public ceremony of shaming. In any case, the custom of levirate marriage has a divine intention: that through man's participation in the birthright, the right of the firstborn, the continuation of the line of the children of Israel with a view to the coming of the seed of Abraham (Gen. 22:18 and Gal. 3:16) would be preserved so the great progeny Christ (the Messiah) may come.

The invoking of levirate marriage in the story of Judah and Tamar is direct evidence that Tamar's action was critical to the fulfillment of God's promise to Abraham in calling him out of Mesopotamia, that he would become a great nation and through his seed the nations of the earth would be blessed.[6] As we will see further on, the handing down of God's promises from Abraham to subsequent generations requires human cooperation in the preservation of bloodlines in the descendants of Abraham. Although Judah was fully aware of his duty, Onan was not similarly inclined (Gen. 38:9-10).

---

6. Actually, this also implies the gift of the land because without the inheritance of the land, Abraham's descendants would never become a great nation, and there would be no way to preserve the continuation of the line of the children of Israel that would eventually lead to Christ. The land is the basic factor upon which the other aspects of God's promise to Abraham become effective. Tamar's action would lead to Perez and further down the line to a notable ancestor, David, through whom the Davidic kingdom would be established. This kingdom would consolidate the children of Israel's hold on the land for a period of Israel's history critical to the building of the temple. And the temple with the functioning priesthood is the focus of Israel as a theocratic nation. This is the partial fulfillment of God's promise to Abraham in shadow in the Old Testament. As opposed to Von Rad, we will argue that interpreting Genesis chapter 38 requires an understanding of God's design in the patriarchal narratives concerning the transmission of God's promise given to Abraham—through man's participation in the birthright.

Enters Tamar:
A woman in
God's plan
With these opening acts as the backdrop, the stage is set for Tamar (v. 6), the human agent through whom God would bring about a reversal in the midst of man's weaknesses and failures. In the eyes of the One who can see the beginning from the end (Rev. 1:8, 21:6, and 22:13), the continuation of God's promise to Abraham concerning the unique seed (Christ) was at risk of being jeopardized because of Judah's condition, a less than stellar situation from which he needed to be extricated.

After his firstborn, Er died, Judah charged his second son, Onan to fulfill his responsibility as a brother-in-law to Tamar (Gen. 38:8) that he may raise up offspring for his brother Er. Onan however knew that the son would not be his, and so he conducted himself selfishly, and as we have seen, God slew him also (vv. 8-10).

Judah fearing now that Shelah, his youngest, would likewise be killed came up with a feeble excuse to save his son. He sent Tamar back to her father's house,[7] seemingly to wait for his son to grow up (v.11), but with little intention of giving Tamar to Shelah (vv. 14, 26). And so through two selfish acts in this drama, that of Judah and his son Onan, Tamar was left with the real possibility of childlessness as her fate.

---

7. G. Von Rad, *The Old Testament Library: Genesis, Revised Edition* (Philadelphia: Westminster Press, 1972), 358. Von Rad commented that only one who was really a widow returned to her father's family (Ruth 1:8ff, Lev. 22:13). Judah's wrong lay in considering this solution as final for himself but presenting it to Tamar as an interim solution.

Tamar's scheme: The second part of the story, an account
A valiant struggle that covered less than one year,[8] slows
for the birthright down the narrative to focus on the action
Tamar took to rectify the situation (vv. 12–30). In her zealousness
to give offspring to her husband, she was spurred to action,
disguising herself as a prostitute in wait for Judah. The Hebrew
word for prostitute here is *qedesa*, a derived word meaning to set
apart or dedicate.[9] According to Canaanite religious practices, the
word was used to designate women set apart for cultic service,
hence temple prostitute.

In the ancient Orient, it was customary in many places for a
married woman to give herself to strangers, because of some
oath, as a sacrifice of chastity.[10] Though temple prostitution was
repulsive to later Israel and forbidden by law, the commonplace
narration here (vv. 15–23), informed by the Canaanite custom
of chastity, seems to suggest that the transaction taking place
was not an unusual scenario in Judah's time. As such, we should
not place undue stress on the modern connotation of the word
"prostitute" with respect Tamar's action. But this incident provides
further incrimination of Judah's questionable condition in his years
in Adullam, particularly so, after the death of his Canaanite wife
(v. 12).

---

8. Tamar's term of pregnancy indicates that this period cannot be much more than nine months.

9. E. H. Merrill, ed., *The Bible Knowledge Key Word Study: Genesis to Deuteronomy* (Colorado Springs: Cook, 2003), 121.

10. G. Von Rad, *Genesis*, 359.

When Tamar saw that Shelah had grown up, but she had not been given to him for marriage, she concocted a plan to regain what is rightfully hers (v. 14). In reading the account, one can't help but be impressed with her determination for she took off her widow's garment, wrapped herself up and sat in wait for Judah at a place that she knew Judah would happen by. Sure enough, her father-in-law passes by, and the protracted negotiation (vv. 15–19) between Judah and her daughter-in-law hints of a keenness of mind on Tamar's part in executing her intention. She realized that the success of her enterprise depended on Judah's admission to culpability and shortcoming in fulfilling his responsibility with respect the right of his firstborn. To ensure that her scheme succeeded, Tamar acquired Judah's signet ring, cord, and staff as a pledge, in lieu of the promised payment of a goat.

According to Herodotus,[11] every Babylonian carried a signet ring and a carved staff as a sort of personal identification. The pledge acquired thus bound Judah personally to Tamar and identified him as the perpetrator in her daughter-in-law's pregnancy (v. 25).

The whole business of Judah's unsuccessful attempt to redeem the pledge later on (vv. 20–23) highlights this as a matter of personal honor for him. It also served to heighten the risk factor for Judah in that he does not want to be put to shame in front of others.

---

11. Ibid., 360.

Judah's Repentance: A successful turnaround—birthright regained

As matters unfold, it was reported to Judah three months later that his daughter-in-law is pregnant through an act of immorality. Immediately Judah pronounced her guilty and commanded those in his presence, "Bring her out, and let her be burned" (v. 24). While Tamar was being brought out, she sent words to her father-in-law that she was pregnant by the man to whom the pledge belongs. To his credit, Judah swiftly recanted (v. 25). When Judah pronounced, "She is more righteous than I, since I did not give her to my son Shelah," (v. 26) in all likelihood he was uttering a word from a repentant heart.[12] The implication is that this sincere repentance—a turnaround initiated by the God who weighs man's heart and effected through Tamar's agency—set Judah on the path that would see him as a notable forbear of Christ. In the meantime, through Tamar's faithfulness and keen presence of mind, her life and that of Judah's unborn son were spared (vv. 28-30).

Hence, contrary to Westermann's view,[13] every part in Genesis 38 contributes to each other and builds toward a climax. After Tamar was spared a cruel fate, she gave birth to Perez (and his

---

12. B. K. Waltke, *Genesis: A Commentary*, 515. Waltke sees this as a turning point for Judah's transformation journey.

13. Westermann's comment that both parts, verses 1 to 11 and 27 to 30 provide details that are not necessary is somewhat puzzling. The link between these parts is supplied by the levirate marriage: verses 1–11 present the background for the invoking of the levirate custom; verses 12 to 26 lay out Tamar's scheme to regain the birthright for her deceased husband, as was her right under the levirate marriage; and finally verses 27 to 30 climaxed with the success of her effort under God's blessing. The levirate marriage as the link between these parts points to this passage's concern for the birthright, the right of the firstborn.

twin Zerah), the son who carried on Judah's line, which will in time lead to David, the notable forbear of the great progeny who would eventually come as God's fulfillment of His promise to Abraham: Christ, the son of David, the son of Abraham (Matt. 1:1).

7. Blessing of Abraham
and the transmission of the birthright

The institution of the levirate custom in Israel, and what is recorded here as the concern for the right of the firstborn[14] in the story of Judah and Tamar, has its beginning in the promise God gave to Abraham. When God told Abraham to leave his home city in Mesopotamia, He said to him, "Go from your country, and from your kindred, and from your father's house to the land that I will show you. And I will make you a great nation, and I will bless you and make your name great, so that you will be a blessing ... and in you all the families of the earth shall be blessed" (Gen. 12:1–3).

Birthright: God's sovereignty and man's responsibility In later development of this theme in Genesis we see the blessing of Abraham passed to Isaac (26:1–5, 24), Abraham's firstborn and also his only son through Sarah. But it was in recounting the handing down of the promise from Isaac to his

---

14. B. K. Waltke, *Genesis: A Commentary*, 492. Waltke considers the section in Genesis that addresses Jacob's descendants (Gen. 37:2–50:26) as also answering the question of who among the twelve sons would have the right of the firstborn.

son Jacob that Scripture first revealed a dynamic of two aspects governing the transmission of the birthright: God's sovereignty and man's responsibility.

According to God's ordination through accepted human custom, Esau as the firstborn of Isaac has the birthright. But in His divine prerogative, God had determined according to His own counsel that Jacob would have the ascendency over his brother Esau (25:23; Rom. 9:13), even though Esau was Isaac's firstborn. This implies that in God's eyes, although Jacob was the second son, he need not strive for the birthright, for it was his regardless of the circumstance of his physical birth.

Yet, not knowing God's determined council, Jacob supplanted, cheated, and strove much of his life. But there is something to be said about Jacob's striving as portrayed in his struggle with his brother Esau to be first, even when the twins were still in their mother, Rebekah's womb (Gen. 25:21-22, 25-26). Later on in life, he would be complicit with his mother's deception of Isaac his father, concerning his brother Esau's birthright— an offense that would see Jacob driven far from home, away from his beloved mother, Rebekah. But the supplanter Jacob had one virtue in the eyes of God. His striving is evidence that he had regard for the birthright as opposed to his brother Esau, who gave it up for some red stew (vv. 30–34; Rom:9:13; Heb. 12:16).

This in no way implies God condoned Jacob's duplicity, for although God had regard for what was in Jacob's heart, He did not let him off lightly. Much rather, in His divine sovereignty, the God of Abraham and Isaac dealt with Jacob throughout much of his adulthood as seen in the record of his life in Genesis (Gen. 37–50). What is clearly portrayed in Jacob's life is that God's ordination goes along with His lifelong dealings. Yes, God did choose him, but Jacob the supplanter needs to be fitted for the birthright that God Himself intended for him. Jacob himself would come to understand this at the end of his life, for he confessed poignantly to Pharaoh nearing the end of his earthly sojourn, "The days of the years of my sojourning are 130 years. Few and evil have been the days of the years of my life, and they have not attained to the days of the years of the life of my fathers in the days of their sojourning" (47:9).

In the Book of Genesis, that birthright was the right for him to be included in the roll call of God as the God of Abraham, Isaac, and Jacob. Thus, from the outset, Scripture lays out the principle that the transmission of the birthright—and the mirror image of personal participation in all that is implied in this blessing—has two unmistakable aspects:

1. God's sovereignty in determining its transmission, and

2. Personal responsibility in partaking of it.

Apart from this realization, we would be hard pressed to ascribe a fitting motivation to Tamar's action, an attribution that must necessarily be in line with Scripture's subsequent high regard accorded her. In fact, from a New Testament perspective, without this insight on the birthright, her eventual place in the genealogy of Jesus Christ (Matt. 1:3) would be most puzzling indeed. In reading Tamar's story, it is all too easy to think that her action was driven by mere human motivation and consideration; perhaps it was the fear of personal loss of inheritance or even the nobler sentiment attributed to this passage by Westermann—the greater good or protecting the community.

Having ruled out divine intentionality, there is little wonder then that Westermann disagreed with the nineteenth century German scholar F. Delitzsch's assessment of Tamar as a great "Old Testament saint." Westermann concluded that theology is not necessary for understanding the narrative, as Tamar was "within her rights,"[15] and that this is all that is necessary for interpreting this unit of God's word. While it cannot be denied that Tamar was within her rights, the exclusive imputation of her action to this motivation alone is a human presumption, it seems to me, that denies Scripture of a divine voice in its own interpretation.

The canonical testimony of Scripture—that voice of God expressed through the community of His people—sees in Tamar's action a higher motivation and purpose than that which Westermann was willing to grant her (see Part 3 for a fuller exposition of the birthright in the canon of Scripture). So to insist on no greater motivation than the preservation of personal

---

15. C. Westermann, *Genesis 37–50*, 52.

human rights is to repudiate the voice of the God who weighs man's hearts.[16]

God initiates but man must respond Besides, it should NOT be forgotten that textual evidence in this passage points unambiguously to God as the One who killed Er and Onan (Gen. 38:7, 10). Therefore, He who sees into man's heart is the One who initiated the crisis in the first place! Why then would this chapter be devoid of divine intentionality? And furthermore, if God had no regard for Er's wickedness and Onan and Judah's selfish actions, why would the same God honor a mere self-directed motive in Tamar's heart, if indeed that was her case?

I contend that it is more in accord with the character of God and Scripture as His word to attribute Tamar's resolve to raise offspring to Judah's firstborn son Er as Tamar's heart for continuity in Israel that is in line with God's promise to Abraham. This calls forth a desire for her participation in the birthright, the right of the firstborn, of which she was meant to have a part. That God recognized and honored Tamar's longing for the birthright is not only evident in His blessing of her action in Genesis 38 but it is

---

16. I am convinced that Scripture cannot be interpreted based on historical or immediate context alone. The task of technical exegesis is necessary, but having done that, the divine intention as seen through the canonical voice of Scripture needs to be brought to bear for a true commentary on any passage. In a practical sense, this means that the significance of a passage needs to be informed by what the entire Scripture has to say on that subject, not in an arbitrary manner, but within the governing vision of God's eternal intention for His creation that runs consistently from Genesis to Revelation. This serves as a beacon in the midst of all the twists and turns caused by many temporary setbacks due to man's failure and or the devil's instigation and stratagem. In this study I have to the best of my ability employed such an approach for the interpretation of Genesis 38.

also testified to by other portions of Scripture, in that her name was much honored in later Israel.

Principle of transferability As is the case with Jacob who sought after the birthright versus his twin brother Esau (who despised it); Tamar's diligence in seeking it in her widowed circumstance once again puts in perspective God's ordination and an individual's responsibility with respect the transmission of the promise God gave to Abraham. Although God has ordained that the firstborn in Israel inherits the birthright, He also desires each person to regard highly their participation in its blessing.

This accounts for the transferability of the birthright first seen in Esau and later in Jacob's firstborn Reuben, among others in the patriarchal narratives. You receive not, because you ask not as it were—a corollary of the New Testament admonition to ask, seek, and knock with regards the promises of God (Matt. 7:7). In Part 5 of this book we will have more to say concerning the New Testament application of the birthright. For now we examine other narrative strands in Genesis (informed by relevant parts of Scripture) that has a direct bearing on the importance of the birthright for the story of Judah and Tamar.

The Book of Genesis reveals that the birthright is transferable but *not in a loose way*. It is governed by scriptural principles in accord with the very nature of God and His desire for mankind. Herein lies the significance of the birthright in the story of Judah and Tamar, and in other portions of patriarchal narratives. The birthright highlights God's sovereignty and an individual's attitude toward His promise. It is a Scriptural dynamic that would characterize the transmission of God's blessing from Abraham, to Isaac, to Jacob, and then Judah and his brothers—a divine and human process that would eventually determine the roll call of those who are in the generation of Jesus Christ (Matt. 1:1–18).

8. The constitution of the birthright

The birthright is the Hebrew *bekorah*,[17] a special portion or entitlement belonging to the right of the firstborn. Among the ancient Jews, bekorah consists of a double portion of whatever the father had to give. It is not merely material possessions,[18] but most importantly, it refers to the covenant blessing of God to Abraham.

The land In the sequence of God's promise to Abraham (Gen. 12:1–3), this would first be the land that God will show him, followed by the promise to make him a great nation and that he would be a blessing to all nations.

In terms of Abraham's responsibility, he was to await the birth of a son that God would give him, but in God's own time. However, having become old and finding themselves still childless, Abraham and Sarah decided that it was high time to help God along by conceiving this son through Hagar, Sarah's Egyptian maid servant

---

17. J. M. Wilson, "Birthright," *The International Standard Bible Encyclopedia*, ed. by James Orr (Peabody MA: Hendrikson, 1994), 478.

18. L. O. Richards, *New International Encyclopedia of Bible Words: Based on the NIV and NASB* (Grand Rapids: Zondervan, 1991), 26.

(16:1-2). In later development—after the birth of Hagar's son, Ishmael—God would appear to Abraham again when he was ninety-nine years old (17:1).

The kingship On that occasion, God corrected Abraham's misdirected hope in Ishmael, his son with Hagar, as the promised seed (vv. 18-20). God specifically reminded Abraham that He would give him a son by Sarah, thus emphasizing that the promised son is not Ishmael (v. 16). He first changed Abraham's name from Abram to Abraham and said to him, "I will make you exceedingly fruitful, and I will make you into nations, and *kings shall come from you*" (v. 6, emphasis added). In this further revelation, we see that to be made into 'nations' is to have 'kings' issuing forth from him.

And in case Abraham missed the point, God also changed Sarai's name to Sarah and reiterated, "I will bless her, and moreover I will give you a son by her. I will bless her, and she shall become nations; *kings of peoples shall come from her*" (17:16, emphasis added). In repeating this promise to Abraham, the stress is that for Sarah to "become nations" is for her descendants "to become kings of peoples." Thus the promise to make Abraham a great nation is also a reference to the "kingship" of Israel, which would find initial fulfillment in the Davidic kingdom in the Old Testament.

The priesthood That Abraham would be a blessing to the nations appears in nascent form in his prayer for Abimelech, which turned God's judgment into blessing (Gen. 20:7, 17–18);

and in Jacob's blessing of Pharaoh nearing the end of Jacob's earthly sojourn (47:7, 10). In the divine concept, to be a blessing to the nations is to have the right and authority to intercede for them. The priesthood[19] stands between God and sinful mankind to intercede for sinful humanity that God's wrath may turn into blessing.

This role, seen first in the patriarchs in embryonic form was intended to be enlarged[20] in the nation of Israel, for further on, God commanded Moses to tell the house of Jacob, "and you shall be to Me a kingdom of priests and a holy nation" (Exod. 19:6). This would be realized in part in the Old Testament in the Aaronic priesthood, but it would ultimately finds fulfillment in Abraham's seed, Christ as the priest according to the order of Melchisedec. In Him God's wrath is averted, for He exists forever to intercede for all who come to Him that He may save them to the uttermost. Thus God's promise to make Abraham a blessing is also a promise concerning the "priesthood" of the house of Jacob.

---

19. The ultimate fulfillment is seen in Abraham's seed: Christ as a priest forever according to the order of Melchisedec (Heb. 5:6). Unlike the Aaronic priesthood, which is terminated upon death, Christ abides forever and so is able to save to the uttermost all those who come forward to God through Him, since He lives always to intercede for them (7:23, 25). Hence He has become the surety of a better covenant (v. 22). In this way, Christ the unique seed, a priest forever according to the order of Melchisedec, fulfills God's promise to Abraham that he would become a blessing to the nations, that is, all those who were once afar but now have been ushered into the better covenant through faith in Christ.

20. God's intention was that Israel be a nation of priests. But the priesthood portion eventually went to the tribe of Levi because of their absoluteness in dealing with the children of Israel who worshipped the golden calf.

In totality God's promise to Abraham concerning the land, a great nation, and a blessing is also a promise concerning the land of Israel, the kingship, and the priesthood of the house of Jacob. Actually, in light of later Scripture, these three aspects of God's promise to Abraham are related: the land is the basis, the territory, the nation from which Israel was meant to exercise her birthright as kings and priests of God in the Old Testament, fulfilling God's promise to Abraham.

9. A quandary in Jacob's line

There is a thought in Scripture that the whole of Israel is God's firstborn. Consequently, this threefold Abrahamic blessing was Israel's birthright as the firstborn[21] of God. That the firstborn in Israel occupy a special place in God's intention is attested to in many places in Scripture (e.g., Exod. 13:2, 15).[22] The birthright and its inheritance by the firstborn would set the Israelites apart as a light to the nations and testify that God is first the God of

---

21. The thought concerning Israel as God's firstborn is initially seen in the special position accorded all firstborn of Israel in God's dealings with them. The note below gives an exhaustive reference to "firstborn" in Scripture. Later, in the New Testament, the Lord Jesus, in answering the Pharisees and scribes, alludes to Israel (as represented by the Pharisees and scribes) as God's firstborn in the parable concerning the prodigal son in Luke 15:11–32.

22. Gen. 4:4; 10:15; 19:31, 33f, 37; 22:21; 25:13; 27:19, 32; 29:26; 35:23; 36:15; 38:6f; 41:51; 43:33; 46:8; 48:14, 18; 49:3; Exod. 4:22f; 6:14; 11:5; 12:12, 29; 13:2, 12f, 15; 22:29; 34:19f; Lev. 27:26; Num. 3:2, 12f, 40ff, 45f, 50; 8:16ff; 18:15, 17; 26:5; 33:4; Deut. 12:6, 17; 14:23; 15:19; 21:15ff; 25:6; 33:17; Josh. 6:26; 17:1; Judg. 8:20; 1 Sam. 8:2; 14:49; 17:13. 2 Sam. 3:2. 1 Kings 16:34. 1 Chron. 1:13, 29; 2:3, 13, 25, 27, 42, 50; 3:1, 15; 4:4; 5:1, 3; 6:28; 8:1, 30, 39; 9:5, 31, 36; 26:2, 4, 10. 2 Chron. 21:3. Neh. 10:36. Job 18:13. Ps. 78:51; 89:27; 105:36; 135:8; 136:10. Isa. 14:30. Jer. 31:9. Ezek. 20:26. Mic. 6:7. Zech. 12:10. Rom. 8:29. Heb. 1:6; 11:28; 12:23.

Abraham, Isaac, and Jacob—not in the sense of particularism,[23] but that God's work on these three men would foreshadow His work on all who would come to Him after the faith of Abraham (Gal. 3:7, 9, 14).

In the progressive unveiling of patriarchal narrative, the blessing of the birthright consisting of:

1. The land (the basis for a nation),

2. The kingship (being a great nation), and

3. The priesthood (being a blessing to others),

would pass from Abraham (Gen. 12:1–3) to Isaac, his only son with Sarah (26:1–5). From Isaac we see it going to Jacob, his second born.

Why?

Esau disqualified According to ordination, Esau, Isaac's firstborn should have inherited the birthright, but due to his profaneness over a bowl of pottage (Gen. 25:31–34; Heb. 12:16), the birthright was transferred to Jacob, who is Isaac's second born. Eventually, although God did bless Esau himself materially (Gen. 33:9), as events played itself out in the writings of Moses (the Pentateuch), we will see that his descendants did not inherit

---

23. W. C. Kaiser, *Mission in the Old Testament: Israel as a Light to the Nations* (Grand Rapids: Baker, 2000), 27–28. Kaiser points to the central message of the seed as one aimed universally at all people, groups and nations from the very beginning. Countering David Filbeck's claim, Kaiser argued, "It was ever and always the plain offer of God to all peoples of the earth through His elected servants of the promise-plan."

any part of the good land, Israel; nor will they participate in the kingship or priesthood of the people of God in the record of the Old Testament.

Reuben defiled   After Jacob the threefold blessing of the promise to Abraham went to Jacob's sons. All of Jacob's sons (with the exception the tribe of Levi who were designated as priests of God) would have a part in that their descendants would eventually have a share in the good land according to tribal allotments. But the right of the firstborn should belong to Reuben. This right refers to a special portion belonging to the firstborn son. That right was taken away from Reuben because of his defilement—for he slept with Bilhah, his father's concubine (Gen. 35:21–23; 1 Chron. 5:21). 1 Chronicles 5:1 says, "The sons of Reuben the firstborn of Israel (for he was the firstborn, but because he defiled his father's couch ... so that he could not be enrolled as the oldest son)." This record gives the explanation for the double portion of the land that was given to Joseph's twin sons, Ephraim and Manasseh, at the time when the children of Israel occupied the good land.

Simeon and Levi cursed   The next in line should have been Simeon and then Levi—Jacob and Leah's second and third sons respectively—but Simeon and Levi[24] were cursed due to their extreme cruelty as seen in their revenge of Dinah, their sister's defilement by Shechem, the son of Hamor (Gen. 34:1-2, 25-30).

---

24. However, the tribe of Levi would eventually redeem themselves due to their absoluteness in their punishment of the idolaters who worshipped the golden calf (Exod. 32:26–29); consequently the priesthood were given to the tribe of Levi (Deut. 33:8–10) on behalf of the children of Israel.

In Jacob's final prophesy concerning his sons, he brought this incident to remembrance and cursed Simeon and Levi's anger and pronounced a judgment on them: "Simeon and Levi are brothers; weapons of violence [cruelty] are their swords. Let my soul not come into their council ... they killed men ... Cursed be their anger, for it is fierce, and their wrath, for it is cruel! I will divide them in Jacob and scatter them in Israel" (49:5–7).

These events transpired within the context of Jacob's personal and family life. In God's hands they were formative for him in that these were among all things that affected him directly from his birth (chapter 25), to his exile from home (chapter 28), his return to his family (chapter 36), and onward to his final days (chapter 50). With the unfolding of the events surrounding the failures of Jacob's sons during the period of Jacob's maturing years, the stage was set for Joseph (chapter 37) and Judah (chapter 38) in this drama concerning the transmission of the birthright in the patriarchal narrative—after the signal failures of his first three sons.

God's dealings with Jacob and his sons were meant to qualify them for the birthright. In this respect, in all stages of Jacob's life, the dynamics of God's sovereignty and man's responsibility is seen to be at work, both in Jacob and his sons. This is revealed firstly in Jacob's fate. The dynamic of this transmission will in turn affect his sons,[25] but that of Joseph, Judah, Reuben, Simeon and Levi would come into particular focus to illustrate a divine principle

---

25. See chart in Appendix F: "Birthright—God's Sovereignty/Man's Responsibility", for a graphic illustration of this principle in God's dealings with the descendants of Jacob mapped against his life.

concerning the birthright. Further down the line, even the fate of Jacob's grandsons Pharez, Zerah, Ephraim, and Manasseh would be affected.

Thus Genesis 38 finds its significance only in the operation of the God of Abraham, Isaac, and Jacob for the birthright in the life of Jacob, and within that the narrative of Joseph, Judah, and Tamar finds its place. When the life of Joseph, starting in Genesis 37, and that of Judah and Tamar in chapter 38 are located within the wider pericope of the story of Jacob (chapters 25 to 50)—with a view to the transmission of the birthright—the intertextual linkages of the stories of Joseph, Judah, and Tamar emerges.

10. Where did the birthright go?

As the proposed outline Appendix A below illustrates, the life of Jacob from Genesis 25 to 50 can be divided into three stages corresponding to his dealings with God:

1. Jacob striving for blessing and being dealt with (chapters 25 to 30),

2. Jacob being broken and depending on God for blessing (chapters 31 to 36), and

3. Jacob maturing and becoming a blessing (chapters 37 to 50).

The birthright in the wider story of Jacob   The first stage shows the transfer of the birthright from Esau to Jacob due to Esau's profanity and

Jacob's regard for it. In the second stage of Jacob's life, certain events transpired—Reuben defiling his father's bed and Dinah being raped by the son of Hamor—that caused Reuben to lose his special right as the firstborn and Jacob's second and third sons, Simeon and Levi to be cursed.

APPENDIX A

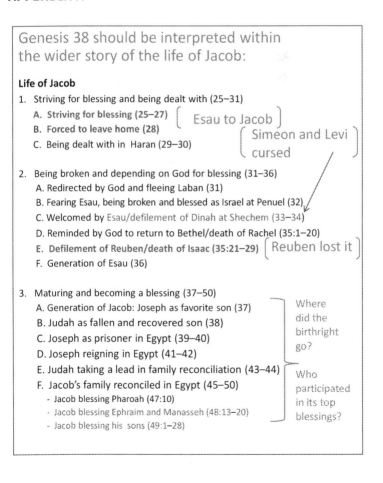

Genesis 38 should be interpreted within the wider story of the life of Jacob:

Life of Jacob

1. Striving for blessing and being dealt with (25–31)
   A. Striving for blessing (25–27)
   B. Forced to leave home (28)
   C. Being dealt with in Haran (29–30)

   Esau to Jacob
   Simeon and Levi cursed

2. Being broken and depending on God for blessing (31–36)
   A. Redirected by God and fleeing Laban (31)
   B. Fearing Esau, being broken and blessed as Israel at Penuel (32)
   C. Welcomed by Esau/defilement of Dinah at Shechem (33–34)
   D. Reminded by God to return to Bethel/death of Rachel (35:1–20)
   E. Defilement of Reuben/death of Isaac (35:21–29)
   F. Generation of Esau (36)

   Reuben lost it

3. Maturing and becoming a blessing (37–50)
   A. Generation of Jacob: Joseph as favorite son (37)
   B. Judah as fallen and recovered son (38)
   C. Joseph as prisoner in Egypt (39–40)
   D. Joseph reigning in Egypt (41–42)
   E. Judah taking a lead in family reconciliation (43–44)
   F. Jacob's family reconciled in Egypt (45–50)
      - Jacob blessing Pharoah (47:10)
      - Jacob blessing Ephraim and Manasseh (48:13–20)
      - Jacob blessing his sons (49:1–28)

   Where did the birthright go?

   Who participated in its top blessings?

In Jacob's maturing years, the third stage of his life, he and his family had returned from the years of exile in Haran. From Haran they went back to Canaan, the land of Abraham and Isaac's sojourning (37:1). The record in chapter 37 focused on a seventeen year old Joseph, and the favoritism bestowed on this son by Jacob. This stirred up the jealousy of Joseph's brothers, resulting in Joseph's sale to Egypt as a slave. The loss of his favorite son caused Jacob's natural affection to be touched in a very deep and personal manner. On top of that, God crowned his work upon Jacob through the devastation of a widespread famine that affected Jacob and his family's survival (chapters 41–42).

When Jacob learned that there were grains in Egypt (42:1), he sent his sons on two separate occasions to acquire sustenance from Egypt. On the first trip one of Jacob's son Simeon, was detained by Joseph (who after many years of slavery, now reigns in Egypt (42:24, 36) as the result of a series of fortuitous events under God's sovereignty). Before his brothers departed for home in Canaan, Joseph charged that they should not appear before him again in Egypt unless they bring their youngest brother Benjamin who was not with them on that first trip.

The second time they went to Egypt was at the height of the famine (43:1). On this occasion they had to bring Benjamin along. As far as Jacob was concerned, he had now lost three sons— Joseph, Simeon and now Benjamin (42:36–38).

All these were Jacob's portion measured out to him by the God of his fathers for his final push toward maturity, that he may be a blessing to all (47:7, 10; and chapter 49). And in God's hands, these seemingly unconnected events in Jacob's life worked out for posterity—for it would answer to whom the double portion of the land, the kingship, and the priesthood would eventually go within the house of Jacob.

11. Birthright: Key to the story of Judah and Tamar

There is a fluidity to the dynamics of the transmission of the birthright that befits God's sovereignty and man's free will. From the perspective of God's sovereignty, it is first a matter of His prerogative. God's prerogative takes precedence over everything else. It was God who decided that Jacob would supersede his brother Esau. From the side of man's choice and responsibility, Esau lost the birthright because of profanity even though it was God's ordination that the birthright was his by virtue of his position according to birth. Reuben would loose the double portion of the land, his right as the firstborn because of profanity and defilement respectively. Simeon would be cursed because of extreme cruelty. But his brother Levi, who was complicit with him in the killing of Hamor and his son Shechem (34:25–26), would find redemption through his descendants in the tribe of Levi in later Israel due to their absoluteness (Exod. 32:26–29; Deut. 33:8–10).[26] That was the incident of the Golden Calf in which the tribe of Levi stepped forward to answer Moses' call to deal harshly with the idolaters. For that service to God, Moses himself would eventually confirm

---

26. Because of the worship of the golden calf and the tribe of Levi's absoluteness in standing with Moses, the priesthood which was originally meant for the nation of Israel was given to the tribe of Levi (Deut. 33:8–9).

that the inheritance of the priesthood goes to the tribe of Levi (Deut. 33:8).

Consequently, with regard to participation in the birthright, each individual also has a part to play. When seen from the perspective of this dynamics, the story of Judah and Tamar has a pivotal role in the patriarchal narratives, for without it we will not know who among Jacob's sons would receive the kingship portion of the threefold blessings of the promise given to Abraham. In this sense, there is confirmation once again that nothing in the divine record is spurious. It is my conviction in studying the word that every detail is there for a reason. The only question is whether we are able to recognize it in God's mercy, or we dismiss it in our ignorance and pride.

Connecting Joseph to Judah Genesis 38 begins with the phrase "It happened at that time ..." (v. 1), which connects the sale of Joseph in chapter 37 to Judah's departure from his brothers to Adullam. The time that Judah spent in Adullam—his marriage to the daughter of the Canaanite Shua, his fathering of three sons, and the arranged marriages of his sons to Tamar—spans approximately twenty-two-plus years.[27]

This coincides with the first twenty-two years of Joseph's life in Egypt (thirteen years in slavery, seven years of reigning during the time of plenty, and two years in the famine). The providential implication, as suggested by Waltke, is that Judah's confession of wrong against Tamar occurs at about the same time as the

27. B. K. Waltke, *Genesis: A Commentary*, 507–508. See Waltke's calculation of the chronology of Genesis 38 in these two pages.

confession of all the brothers in their wrong against Joseph (compare 38:26 with 42:21).

Qualifying Judah for the kingship After Judah repented, we see him back again with his brothers. During the years that famine ravaged Egypt, Judah's role was bound up with that of Joseph.[28] While Joseph took the lead in preserving the house of Jacob in Egypt, a recovered Judah took the lead among his brothers in reconciling Jacob's family. And Joseph, for his purity and role in the preservation of the children of Israel during the famine would receive the birthright of a double portion of the land through his two sons, Ephraim and Manasseh (39:7–20, 48:13–16, 49:3–4; 1 Chron. 5:1).

But some questions yet remain.

Who inherits the kingship portion of the blessing? Through whose line would God's sovereignty act across the centuries until the promised seed, the Messiah comes?

And why was Judah chosen rather than someone else..?

As the table in Appendix B below illustrates, the answer is in the story recorded in Genesis 38.

---

28. See chart in Appendix G: "Time Extent of Genesis 38" for a graphic illustration of God's providential arrangement in synchronizing Joseph's role with that of Judah's to effect the preservation and reconciliation of the house of Jacob.

APPENDIX B

The story of Judah in Genesis: with Genesis 38 serving as a pivot for recovery

Caption	Key Verses	Comment
Judah's birth and position	Gen. 29:35, 35:23	Judah is Jacob's fourth son through his wife Leah.
Role in Joseph's betrayal	Gen. 37:26–28	Judah proposed the sale of Joseph to the Ishmaelites.
Falling away	Gen. 38:1–11	Judah departed from his brothers, befriended an Adullamite and married a Canaanite.
Repentance and recovery	Gen. 38:12–20	Judah repented with the words, "She is more righteous than I ..." (v. 26).
Leading role in family reconciliation	Gen. 43:1–8, 44:1–34, 46:12, 28	During the famine Judah first pledged himself to Jacob as surety; and again to Joseph as replacement for Benjamin's release.
The approval of Judah in Jacob's prophesy concerning his sons	Gen. 49:8–12	"The scepter shall not depart from Judah, nor the ruler's staff from between his feet, until tribute comes to him; and to him shall be the obedience of the peoples" (v. 10).

Judah's pathway to inheriting the kingship is best seen in twenty-five scriptural references in the book of Genesis: 29:35; 35:23; 37:26; 38:1f, 6, 8, 11f, 15, 20, 22ff, 26; 43:3, 8; 44:14, 16, 18; 46:12, 28; and 49:8 forward. Among these occurrences, close to half (twelve verses) are found in Genesis 38. When cast in the format above, the captions I provided for these verses tell a story of the redeeming grace of God in Judah's falling away and recovery that is quite unmistakable. Tamar's action in Genesis 38 plays a critical role in this turnaround. The story of Judah and Tamar is certainly a watershed for Judah.

Without this story in Genesis 38:

1. Judah would not have recovered from his falling away

2. There would be no one suitable to lead the reconciliation among his brothers at the height of the famine

3. There would be a gap in the caring for Jacob's heart in his old age, and

4. No one would have been qualified to inherit the kingship portion of the promise of Abraham

And so for her role as God's agent in effecting these turnarounds—at a time when the preservation of the line of Judah was at risk—Tamar's name would be much honored in later Israel (Ruth 4:12–13), and she would take her place for all time in the generation of Jesus Christ, the son of David, the son of Abraham (Matt. 1:1, 3).

As for Judah (fallen but chosen of God)—the very man who betrayed his brother Joseph—he was destined to "prevail" over his brothers in effecting Jacob's family reconciliation. Regarding this role, Scripture would declare in Genesis 49:10, "The scepter shall not depart from Judah, nor the ruler's staff from between his feet, until tribute comes to him; and to him shall be the obedience of the peoples." Seen in this light, Genesis 38 is pivotal in God's operation among the descendants of Jacob to turn adversity into triumph, and in the process portray for all generations the kind of person that God could and would use to inherit the kingship blessing of the birthright (Gen. 49:8–11; 1 Chron. 5:1–2), a portion of the threefold blessing of the birthright that in time would usher in the great progeny—a Son who would rule the universe.[29]

Pivotal position of Genesis 38   The intertextual integrity of the story of Judah and Tamar within the life of Jacob, and by extension the rest of patriarchal narratives, is thus demonstrated from the deep structure of the book of Genesis, through the dynamics of the transmission of the birthright. With this in mind, all that remains is to present the cohesion within the story in relation to Jacob's maturing years. This is best illustrated by expanding the outline of Genesis 38 within the events that would shape Jacob's maturity in his final years.

From this perspective, the story of Judah and Tamar within the life of Jacob in his maturing years divides naturally into two cohesive parts:

1.   Judah's falling away after betraying Joseph (Gen. 38:1–11),

2.   His recovery through Tamar's faithfulness (vv. 12–30),

These two motifs in Genesis 38 concerning Judah's falling away and recovery fit in with the other events God sovereignly arranged around Jacob in his last years for his final perfecting so he would

---

29. Ibid., 508. This phrase is borrowed from Waltke.

become a blessing to all—and in this even Pharaoh himself, the Gentile head of a powerful ancient empire was not excepted. According to Hebrews, it is beyond dispute that the lesser is blessed by the greater (Heb. 7:7).

APPENDIX C

Outlining Genesis 38

3. Life of Jacob: Maturing and becoming a blessing (37–50)
   A. Generation of Jacob: Joseph as favorite son (37)
   B. Judah as fallen and recovered son (38:1–30)
   1. Fall away after betraying Joseph (vv. 1–11)
      a. Departing from his brothers (v. 1)
      b. Marrying a Canaanite and fathering sons (vv. 2–5)
      c. Judah's sons and Tamar—violating Levirate marriage, putting participation in birthright at risk (vv. 6–11)

   2. Recover through Tamar's faithfulness (vv. 12–30)
      a. Tamar's unseemly scheme for participation in birthright (vv. 12–19)
      b. Tamar's vindication due to her faithfulness – Judah's confession(vv. 20–26)
      c. Participation in birthright gained: Pharez and Zerah (vv. 27–30)
   C. Joseph as prisoner in Egypt (39–40)
   D. Joseph reigning in Egypt(41–42)
   E. Judah taking a lead in family reconciliation (43–44)
   F. Jacob's family reconciled in Egypt: (45–50)
      - Jacob blessing Pharaoh (47:10)
      - Jacob blessing Ephraim and Manasseh (48:13–20)
      - Jacob blessing his sons (49:1–28)

As presented in the outline in Appendix C above, the first section of Jacob's maturing years introduces his favorite son, Joseph, whose "death" (for it was so to Jacob) would be a major personal loss. God used that loss to fully transform the man from a conniving supplanter to one who was a blessing to others. In the second section, running parallel with Joseph's slavery in Egypt, Judah falls away after betraying Joseph. Through Tamar's faithfulness, he was recovered and went back to be with his brothers. At the height of the famine, while Joseph was reigning in Egypt, Judah took the lead among his brothers in family reconciliation. As a result, the house of Jacob was reunited again with Joseph in Egypt.

During Jacob's final sojourn in Egypt, we see the high point of God's work on him. The man Jacob had rightly become Israel, not just in position or name only but also dispositionally. The scheming, conniving, and supplanting Jacob is no longer visible in the narrative. He has become a blessing to people around him, both within and without the house of Jacob—Pharaoh, Ephraim, Manasseh, and his twelve sons—all were blessed by him!

Section summary   The first mention of levirate marriage in Scripture is in Genesis 38, in the story of Judah and Tamar. The meaning of this custom is that the firstborn son of the levir with his sister-in-law shall succeed to the name of the dead brother, that his name may not be blotted out of Israel. This custom has a primarily divine intention in that, through the continuation of the firstborn, the line of Israel with a view to the great progeny would be preserved. The first mention of the levirate custom here is a direct allusion to an overriding concern for the birthright, the right of the firstborn in this story within the life of Jacob.

Even in the Old Testament, among the ancient Israelites the birthright is not firstly related to material possessions. It pertains to God's promise to Abraham concerning the land, becoming a great nation (kingship), and a blessing (priesthood). From the vantage point of God's promise, the story of the patriarchs can be viewed as God's dealings with Abraham, Isaac, and Jacob and his descendants to effect a transmission of the birthright according to a two-sided principle of God's sovereignty and an individual's responsibility. Through this dynamic operating in the deep structure of the patriarchal narratives, the birthright went from Abraham to Isaac and then to Jacob.

Genesis 38, the story of Judah and Tamar, serves as a bridge to address the question concerning the transmission of the kingship portion of God's threefold promise to Abraham, a blessing Reuben lost when he defiled his father's bed. With the subsequent disqualification of Simeon and Levi, the narrative in Jacob's life now focuses on Judah, intertwined with that of Joseph's story. In these two men, the God of Abraham, Isaac, and Jacob would show His kindness by recovering a fallen Judah (who betrayed Joseph) through Tamar's faithfulness. In the process, God worked out the reconciliation and preservation of the house of Jacob through these two brothers, Judah and Joseph.

And so, when seen from the perspective of the dynamics of the birthright in God's dealings with the patriarchs Abraham, Isaac, and Jacob, Genesis 38 is not an insertion devoid of intratexual cohesion and intertextual integrity as some scholars perceive. Rather, the story of Judah and Tamar is pivotal for it addresses the recovery of Judah through Tamar intratextually. And intertextually, with respect to the other patriarchal narratives, it answers the question concerning who would eventually receive the portion of kingship in God's promise to Abraham. Judah's participation in that blessing would lead to God's fulfillment of His promise in the person of Jesus Christ, in whom all the promises of God to Abraham's posterity is a resounding yes! (2 Cor. 1:20).

Part 3: Back to the Present

Overview

Part 3 is an excursus which surveys the basis for a Christian reading of Genesis 38 that holds in highest regards the Bible as authoritative and normative for Christians. This involves a grasp of the authority of the final form of the canon of Scripture. The character of Christian Scripture as a two-testament witness to the incarnation of God in Christ must be brought to bear—and an approach that the church fathers understood as the rule of faith is necessary for an authentic Christian reading of the first Testament. Such a ruled reading sees the hidden life of a pre-incarnated Christ in the first Testament that carries forward to its fulfillment in the present in the incarnated Christ of God in the second Testament.

Section Outline

Part 3: Back to the Present

Section Introduction

12. The subversive example of Jesus
- o   Learning from Jesus
- o   Incarnation and Scripture reading

13. A Christian reading of Scripture
- o   Based on Christ's preexistence
- o   Seeing the imprint of who Jesus is

14. Scripture and the community of faith
- o   Recovering the function of Scripture
- o   Canonical formation
- o   Canonical shaping
- o   Canonical interpretation
- o   Child's normative canon
- o   Transcending historical boundaries

15. The character of Christian Scripture and the rule of faith
- o   Significance of the rule of faith
- o   Christ is the coherence across both Testaments

16. 'Judah and Tamar' in a two-testament approach
- o   A ruled reading in the transmission of kingship

Section Summary

Back to the Present

Section Introduction

How should Christians enter into the story of Judah and Tamar in a way that respect both Testaments of sacred Scripture? Specifically, what in God's work in the first Testament with regard to transmission of the birthright and reconciliation of the house of Jacob carries over to the New Testament's realization of Jesus as the fulfillment of God's promise to Abraham? The answer to this seemingly innocuous question belies a subversive understanding of the Old and New Testament according to an apostolic sanctioned interpretation that takes Christ as the center of God's actions across Scripture. While it is the fashion for various adherents to claim that the Bible is one, the fact is there are as many readings of Scripture as there are communities of faith that hold it as authoritative.

12. The subversive example of Jesus

In Jesus' time the Pharisees read the first Testament differently. On one Sabbath, Jesus provoked the ire of the Pharisees when He took His disciples through the grainfields, and they began to pick the heads of the grain and eat because they were hungry (Matt. 12:1). In answer to the Pharisees' accusation that His disciples were breaking the law of the Sabbath (v.2), Jesus directed them to the actions of David and the priests in the temple. He pointed out that David entered the house of God and ate the bread of the Presence when he was running from Saul, even though it was not lawful for him and his followers to eat except the priests. Moreover, the priests themselves profane the Sabbath but were guiltless because they acted within the confine of the temple (performed their priestly duties) during the Sabbath (vv. 3–5).

Learning from Jesus Jesus' defense of the action of His disciples contains a subversive element in that it harbors a thinking that is alien to the Pharisees. Jesus sees Himself as the fulfillment of the first Testament, the details of which portrays Him as the reality. He is the king for whom David is the shadow. He is also greater than the temple. If David was not held to account, then neither can Jesus be. If the temple absolved the priests for acting on the Sabbath, then Jesus' disciples are guiltless for they acted in the presence of the One who is the greater temple. The logic follows—for if the lesser is guiltless in profaning the Sabbath, then Jesus and His followers are also guiltless for He is Lord of the Sabbath (v. 5). Even as day follows night, the coming of Jesus requires a reorientation of the reading of the Old Testament in light of His presence in the New.

Incarnation and Scripture Reading The incarnation of God in Christ dictates a view of Scripture that is centered solely on the beloved Son of God. On the day of transfiguration Peter, James and John saw Moses and Elijah talking to Jesus. When Peter wanted to build three tents: one for Moses (the representative of the law), one for Elijah (as representative of the prophet), a bright cloud overshadowed them, and a voice out of the cloud said, "This is my beloved Son, with whom I am well pleased; listen to him" (Matt. 17:5). Thereafter, Moses and Elijah promptly disappeared, and only Jesus remained (v. 8). Listening to Jesus would in time entail the emergence of a second Testament witness to complete the first. The New Testament is the record of the voice of the beloved Son of God concerning whom Moses and Elijah (that is the entire law and the prophets in the first Testament) have directed their join witness. And to this second witness, God has given charge that His people hear only Him.

Jesus Himself said, "You search the Scriptures because you think that in them you have eternal life; and it is they that bear witness about me, yet you refuse to come to me that you may have life" (Matt. 5:39-40). Without Jesus as the content and subject of the second Testament, the first would be devoid of the life that God has appointed for His people. Therefore, it should come as no surprise that when a resurrected Jesus interpreted to the two disciples on the road to Emmaus all things concerning Himself from the Scripture (Luke 24:27)—He was making an astounding claim in that He was explicitly referencing events recorded in the first Testament (Moses and all the Prophets) as His move before His incarnation that points forward to its fulfillment in Himself in His incarnation event.

13. A Christian reading of Scripture

The eyes of Christian faith view the second Testament as the fulfillment of the first through the lens of Jesus' incarnation, human life, crucifixion, resurrection, ascension, outpouring of the Spirit, and indwelling of the believers as His body—consummating in His second coming at the end of the age. This is the unique purpose of God's actions across the two Testaments of Christian Scripture, and so a Christian reading of the story recorded in Genesis 38 sees God's intention in Christ foreshadowed there.

Based on Christ's preexistence Christian faith informs us it is the same God who is revealed in both Testaments. This necessarily implies that God's pre-incarnational acts in Christ in the Old Testament prefigure His move in the second—in the person of Christ's advent. Everything that Christ is and does as the second of the divine Trinity is God's move. Christ's preexistence from eternity to eternity as the Son in the Godhead ensures His centrality in God's acts in the divine record of Genesis 38. Hence a Christian reading of what transpired in the story of Judah and Tamar must seek out key aspects of Christ as the One to whom the entire first Testament points.

Indeed, the New Testament's assertion that Christ is the be all and end all of God's actions across Scripture (Luke 24:27, John 5:39–40, Rom. 10:4) is astonishing. Taken to heart, it means that whatever characterizes God's actions in Christ as recorded in the Old Testament is applicable to New Testament believers in the sense that the recorded events of ancient Israel follows the same pattern of God's action in Christ as revealed in the second Testament. In the eyes of Him who is the Alpha and the Omega, the beginning and the end (Rev. 1:8; 21:6), the artifacts of the entire first Testament "... are a shadow of the things to come, but the substance belongs to Christ" (Col. 2:17).

Seeing the imprint of who Jesus is
We see in the Old Testament an imprint of who Christ is in the New. The God of Abraham, Isaac and Jacob who acted in the lives of the patriarchs follows the pattern of God's action in Christ in the New Testament. It is the God of Abraham, Isaac and Jacob as manifested in Christ who guarantees the continuity and applicability of His words and actions across both Testaments. As such, the apostle Paul boldly carries forward the experiences of the children of Israel with God—in Egypt, the crossing of the Red Sea, their wondering in the wilderness—and applies it to the believers' baptism and living in Christ in the church today (1 Cor. 10:1–11). Regarding this way of interpretation, even the apostle Peter concurs, for he acknowledged wholeheartedly that in all of Paul's letters, "... there are some things in them hard to understand, which the ignorant and unstable twist to their own destruction; as they do the other Scriptures" (2 Pet. 3:16). This confession, in effect, gives apostolic authority to a second Testament's reading of itself as the fulfillment of the first, for the extensive writings of Paul makes clear that he sees it as such.

With this observation as preliminary, how should we appropriate the inheritance of the kingship in the story of Judah and Tamar in Genesis 38 from a Christian perspective? Any proposed reading should uphold the integrity of the first Testament in its own right. We are obliged to start with Moses and Elijah for it is they who first give witness to God's intention in Christ; yet a Christian reading is one which morphed into Jesus alone as the One who remains (Matt. 17:8). Such a reading assumes the unity of both Testaments of Scripture that has been called into question by modern critical scholarship. Among the varied apparatus of biblical criticism, that of Brevard Child's "canonical approach" attempts to return interpretive authority to the final form of scriptural text. Though Childs cannot be regarded as conservative in his position on fundamental Christian conception of revelation; his recommended approach does shed some light on the formation of Scripture as the canonical voice of God in the community of believers. The word "canonical" as used here is a derivative of the Greek word for canon which means "standard or measuring rod." The canon of Scripture is that which delineates the standard that the church used in receiving the Word of God.

14. Scripture and the community of faith

Having learnt of Jesus, the apostles amplify a Christ-centered reading of the Old Testament in their writings to the new community of faith. Behind their appropriation of the first Testament as authoritative for Christians is an assumption of continuity guaranteed by God's action in Christ in shaping Scripture, Israel and the church. God first acted in Christ's pre-incarnation in the life of the patriarchs. What was eventually recorded in Israel's Scripture concerning God was superintended by the very God of Abraham, Isaac and Jacob for the constitution of Israel as a community of faith that would bear fruit in the fullness of time— in the coming of the seed of Abraham, Christ (Gal. 4:4). In this sense both Israel's Scripture and her constitution as a community subsist in the God of their fathers whose intention it was to give life to both (Israel and her Scripture) as a witness to the One who was to come.

The voice of Jesus in the second Testament is for the formation of an extended new community centered on Himself as the Christ of God. Concerning this Jesus said, "And I have other sheep that are not of this fold. I must bring them also, and they will listen to my voice. So there will be one flock, one shepherd" (John 10:16). As such, the apostolic way of reading Scripture gives credence to what Jesus had promised His disciples while He was yet with them, "I still have many things to say to you, but you cannot bear them now. When the Spirit of truth comes, he will guide you into all the truth, for he will not speak on his own authority, but whatever he hears he will speak, and he will declare to you the things that are to come. He will glorify me, for he will take what is mine and declare it to you" (John 16:12-14). Certainly the record of the New Testament as the extension of the voice of the Spirit bears witness to this promise of Jesus' continued speaking in the apostles' writing ministry to the churches as the new community of faith.

Recovering the function of Scripture The rise of classic historical criticism with its emphasis on tracing the dubious human origins of what goes into the final text of Scripture have missed the function God intended Scripture to have, that is to shape the formation and direction of the community of faith. An approach pioneered by Brevard Childs deals with this in some way—particularly his emphasis on the development, process, and continuing relevance of the canon of Scripture for the community. While it has been argued that Childs vest too much authority for Scripture's meaning in the confessing community—our tacit assumption in this book in appropriating his reader-centered reading for Genesis 38 is that God's sovereign action in the community of faith is the basis for the formation of Scripture. As such the confessing community ultimately derives its authority from God via the Scripture that shapes its formation.

While there is a human process to canonical formation, shaping and interpretation—all these activities were guided, inspired, and superintended at every point by the God who gives rise to the community and the final text captures His intention and interactions with them. There is a divine and human dimension that goes into every detail of the shaping of the canon of Scripture across one thousand five hundred years of its development from Genesis to Revelation. Let's begin by looking at a few basic elements on the formation and shaping of the canon, for it has a bearing on our reading of the story of Judah and Tamar as Christian Scripture.

In the early seventies and eighties, Brevard Childs pioneered his distinctive Old Testament interpretation that he called the canonical approach—with particular emphasis on the authority of the final form of the text of Scripture (the canon of Scripture) as it has been handed down to us. Childs saw his own effort as a challenge to many established approaches to Old Testament criticism that places undue emphasis on speculative changes that texts may have undergone over time (diachronistic effects) before they supposedly reach the final form that we have today. James A. Sanders later developed an alternative that incorporates what scholars consider as diachronistic changes in texts over time in dialog with Childs' work—an approach Sanders called canonical criticism.

But for the pragmatic purpose of this book, we will take canonical criticism to be that intended by Childs' original work, for the very reason that the text of the Bible that we hold in our hands is what we have in its final form. From this perspective, whatever came before the final accepted canon of Scripture are man's educated guesses at best, and at worse a distortion of what God intended for the Church to receive as Christian Scripture. What follows is a brief summary of this approach to set the context for a discussion on a proposed reading of the story of Judah and Tamar in Genesis 38 that respects God's actions in Christ across both Testaments.

Canonical formation Imagine if you will, the exodus of the children of Israel from Egypt. The exodus account consisted of a sequence of significant events that involved the Israelites as a community of faith, which produced the biblical text.[1] The original event had a strong influence on the community, for through it the children of Israel experienced God in a special and powerful way. This event became part of the common knowledge of the community that was either remembered and orally transmitted or written down. In some sense the event becomes a way for them to understand God and a way to communicate about God, so an initial body of materials may have developed around it that we may call a protocanon.

Later, in their crossing of the Red Sea and journeying in the wilderness, other events happened. These were added to the protocanonical base. During the Israelites' forty years of journeying and fighting in the wilderness, many more events transpired. When these occurred, a small body of protocanon would have existed that had become a rudimentary interpretive framework. Thus their present experience could be described in categories already acquired, and these were added to the community's body of knowledge about God. More and more works were added in this way to the small protocanon. In time a larger body of work developed, and as it continued to influence the life of faith in the community, it could be shaped into larger

1. The Pentateuchal narratives have been used here as an example for illustrative reasons; the sole purpose of which is to concretize the discussion. It is not a statement on the actual canonical process and shaping of the Pentateuch but only the principle as such. The establishment of the actual process is a matter for the relevant textual scholars to argue over. Besides, Childs rightly noted that editors may have done their best to obscure their identity, and thus the actual process of canonical formation is not clearly discernable. This seems to me to be a compelling reason for accepting his conviction that final authority should be vested only in the normative canon for the task of exegesis.

epics or linked narratives by an author, or redactor as some would have it.

Canonical shaping The process just described has been called canonical shaping. Canonical shaping may also include updating activities, which was required to reflect the way the material communicated to the community, and that may have changed over time. But at some point the canon would have reached a degree of stability and have become established as expressing an accepted understanding for the community under God's sovereign direction. When that happened, additions to the canon stopped since the canon was seen to be sufficiently rich to communicate what was important about God. Either that or the community saw dangerous deviations from its accepted tradition and therefore protected its canon by describing its limit accurately. The point is, from then on only minor fluctuations in the texts occurred. From that time forward the canon became static and could no longer be reshaped to communicate to new historical or linguistic situations since the canon had become fixed.

Canonical interpretation While the canon may remain static, over time a body of interpretive knowledge developed around the canon to preserve its meaning for future generations. That interpretive body of knowledge is also used to make the content of the canon applicable to contemporary situations. In some way, this interpretive body gives back to the canon a certain degree of flexibility, which it lost through fixation when it was canonized. And so, armed with this canon and an interpretive framework, when a future event happens, it is interpreted in the context of the canon utilizing the interpretive framework. In this sense, the canon speaks to a future generation and is applicable in a different historical and cultural context. Although the canon came from a different time and situation, it is not historically bound but continues to be normative (the authoritative measure) for understanding God. In this way the canon continues to be influential for future generations.

Childs' normative canon Childs is the forerunner in this approach. He pioneered the field, and it is not too much to observe that all the literature in this area developed in dialog with what he had initially laid down. Childs' work *Introduction to the Old Testament as Scripture* showcases this new approach to understanding the Old Testament. There he takes issue with the nature of the Bible's historical actuality.[2] Childs' stated aim was to improve the study of the Bible by redefining the relationship between historical critical methods and its theological use within the community of faith. He wished to transcend the classical distinction between liberal and conservative.

He did this by changing the way the historical nature of the Bible is viewed (a new hermeneutic) in order to do justice to the nature of Israel's unique history. Israel's understanding of God developed over time, and the text of the Old Testament gives witness to this process. Thus Israel's literature needs to be treated with respect for its own integrity. These writings are both historically and

---

2. B. S. Childs, *Introduction to the Old Testament as Scripture* (Philadelphia: Fortress Press, 1979), 71.

theologically conditioned and have to be treated as such. The biblical text reflects the history of the encounter between God and Israel.[3]

Transcending historical boundaries Childs shares his concern with newer literary critics of accepting the text's integrity on its own terms, apart from the classic diachronistic reconstruction in historical criticism using "scientific criteria." For Childs the final form of the text (the canonical text) is the ultimate measure for the understanding of the Old Testament. Only in the final form has the accepted history of Israel with God reached an end, and only in the final form can the full effect of revelatory history be perceived. It is the final text that continues to be authoritative for the community of faith and not any earlier ones. This would mean that only Scripture after canonization is authoritative, but none of the earlier protocanonical stages are.[4]

What is important is that the canonical process led to messages bound to a historical situation becoming actualized for different historical circumstances, and in this manner those messages transcended historical bounds. But editors may have done their best to obscure their identity, and thus the actual process of canonical formation is not clearly discernable. But the Scripture thus formed would in time come to redefine Israel as a people. Consequently, the canon and the community cannot be separated.

---

3. Ibid., 15, 71, 73.

4. Ibid., 74–76.

So Childs criticized the classical, historical critical method for failing to relate the canonical writings correctly to the community of faith. In his view, the identity of the community shaped the canonical writings and vice versa. Modern critical methods usually assume the historical reference is key to interpretation, forgetting all about the role Scripture has played in the community of faith. Childs sees his canonical approach as setting the limit on interpretive tasks by taking traditional parameters seriously,[5] but the normative canon as reflected in the Scripture we received is the platform to start exegesis.[6]

15. The character of Christian Scripture and the rule of faith

What Childs had done was to vest authority in the final form of Scripture through an understanding of its formation, shaping and interpretation. While Childs may have overly vested the foundation for authority or meaning of Scripture with the community, I hold that there is nothing inherent in this view that necessarily rejects God's active participation in the community. From a conservative position, these processes are not just human undertakings. They assume a dimension that goes beyond human limitations to a divine intentionality in the text for the community's formation and shaping. Three decades have gone by since Childs pioneered his approach. In that time many have been the proponents and detractors who have added their voices

---

5. B. S. Childs, *Old Testament Theology in Canonical Context* (Philadelphia: Fortress Press, 1986), 78–79, 82.

6. ———, *Introduction to the Old Testament as Scripture*, 41, 78–82.

to Childs' stated agenda.[7] In Christopher Seitz's recent work (2011) on theological interpretation,[8] *The Character of Christian Scripture: The Significance of a Two-Testament Bible*, he defended Childs' canonical approach and stressed that this offers the most compelling, comprehensive account of biblical interpretation and theology presently offered.

After addressing various objections by carefully looking at the nuances of these criticisms in chapter 1 of his book, Seitz reaffirmed that a canonical approach is essential to doing biblical theology. Chapter 2 examines the nature of biblical theology in relation to a canonical approach. There Seitz wrote, "Christian theological reflection on the canon of Scripture as twofold in essence is the main task of biblical theology." He went on to clarify that "use of the Old Testament by the New is not a substitute for Christian theological reflection on the Old Testament in its own formal integrity." The continuity of the second Testament with the first is predicated upon the integrity of the first Testament in its own right.

---

7. It is beyond the scope, not to mention the competence, of this present study to go into these. Suffice it here to highlight a key critique by Sanders that Childs's normative canon severs the connection between historical reality and the canon. Child's reply is that the canonical context appropriates the historical material in a variety of ways, which is sometimes loose. The canonical context "bears witness to a representative reality, which transcends any given historical situation. At other times the canonical context works historical material into its very core and makes full use of a public witness to common historical reality ... The canonical process is, in no way, divorced from the historical process ... but the two processes retain their own integrity and are not to be fused" (Birch, Birch, Bruce C., D. A. Knight, J. L. Mays, D. P. Polk, J. A. Sanders, and B. S. Childs, *Horizons in Biblical Theology* vol. 2 (1980), 203). Childs certainly seems to see some importance in connections between historical reality and the canon.

8. C. R. Seitz, *The Character of Christian Scripture; the Significance of a Two-Testament Bible* (Grand Rapids: Baker Academics, 2011), 94–96, 179–181.

The book proceeded in chapter 5 to make clear how the Old and New Testament fit into a canonical approach, in such a way that both testaments should be allowed to sound their own "theological notes." In his view, biblical theology should deal in a balanced and appropriate way with the dual voice of Christian Scripture, both New and Old Testament. Seitz concludes the book with the "rule of faith," as key to interpretations that emphasize the importance of treating the New and Old Testament as equals in a two-testament Bible.

Significance of the rule of faith In Seitz's view, the so-called rule of faith needs to be properly understood to appreciate the character of Christian Scripture hermeneutically [9](that is, for interpretation and preaching). This is not a kind of Reader's Digest condensation or retelling, in which the Old Testament message is used chiefly to describe crucial or preliminary episodes prior to Christ's advent. The essence of the rule is based on a proper identification of what the church fathers called the 'hypothesis' of Scripture, and an assumption of this, in the area of 'order' (*taxis*) and 'arrangement' or connection (*hiermas*).[10] The challenges presented to the ante-Nicene fathers imply that a catholic, Christian "ruled reading" of the first Testament (Law, Prophets,

---

9. Ibid., 191–199.

10. Ibid., 195.

and Writings) was ultimately impossible.[11] That is, the Old Testament is incomplete without the emergence of a second Testament witness—the New Testament canon to describe the apostolic limits and public character of Christian claims as *tota Scriptura*.

Christ is the coherence across both Testaments This would entail an understanding or perception of how the order and larger coherence can be grasped across the two-Testament witness of Christian Scripture. In this reading, the subject of Scripture is brought to bear, and this subject is the creator God, with whom the Son is eternally related. The Scripture gives the Holy Spirit the opportunity to declare this through the economies and episodes of God's ways in and with Israel. So the rule of faith is "the scripturally grounded articulation, based upon a proper perception of the *hypothesis* (emphasis added) of Scripture, that Jesus Christ is one with the God who sent him and who is active in the Scriptures inherited, the Holy Spirit being the means of testifying to his active, if hidden life

---

11. As Seitz points out, the challenges faced by the ante-Nicene fathers (as seen in their defense against many erroneous readings) imply that the first Testament was (1) insufficient, (2) misleading or useful only to show a wrong theological way, (3) in need of further testimony given to special teachers, or (4) positive in range and potential but only because it can be aligned with all kinds of new revelations. Consequently, a Christian perception of Scripture requires the completion of a second Testament to circumscribe the various readings and meanings according to a central subject in *tota Scriptura*. The "subject" is the creator God as manifested through the activities of the pre-incarnated Son, who is always one with the Father in His move in the Old Testament. God is made manifest in the New Testament by the move of Jesus Christ as the incarnated One and subsequently the apostles as they were one with the Son. The move of God across both Testaments of Christian Scripture is testified to by the Holy Spirit utilizing the canon of Christian Scripture.

in the 'Old Testament' and our apprehension of that."[12] In this way the rule guards against and rules out alternatives that have failed to recognize the order and coherence of the Scriptures in their totality as speaking of Christ. It stipulates that the work of Christ is in various economies before His incarnation, alongside the Scripture's speaking both of Christ's first and second advents.

In this, Daniel J. Treier agrees, for he has previously stated that the rule of faith "is an appeal to objective canonical unity based on God's use of the scriptural texts to bear witness to Christ."[13] Treier noted that among the themes that surfaced for the church fathers, the rule of faith is a basic summary of the biblical story centered on identifying God to be Triune—Father, Son, and Holy Spirit. Consequently, an interpretation guided by the rule of faith tells the story of the *Triune God*.[14]

In a more recent work, Joel B. Green observed that this is indeed one of the main characteristics of the early followers of Christ, for they read "Scriptures in a certain way, working with hermeneutics that located the advent, life, ministry, death, and resurrection of Jesus Christ as the focal point of God's aim in creation and exodus."[15] The work of these scholars addressed a key note: *regula fidei* (rule of faith) is what distinguishes a Christian reading

---

12. Ibid., 198.

13. D. J. Treier, *Introducing Theological Interpretation of Scripture: Recovering a Christian Perspective* (Grand Rapids: Baker Academics, 2008), 114.

14. Ibid., 57, 59.

15. J. B. Green, *Practicing Theological Interpretation: Engaging Biblical Texts for Faith and Formation* (Grand Rapids: Baker Academics, 2011), 73.

of Israel's Scripture (rather than say, a Pharisaic or Essene or any other readings), in that it applies certain theological lenses by which the followers of Christ have identified the God of Abraham, Isaac, and Jacob with the God who raised Jesus from the dead. These are Christological lenses by which Jesus' followers "have understood that Israel's Scriptures speak of Christ and then the restoration of God's people in the work of Christ such that the church, composed of Jew and gentile, finds its own history within the pages of these Scripture."[16]

16. 'Judah and Tamar' in a two-testament approach

It is in this mold of canonical approach as suggested by Childs (in the sense of vestment of authority in the final form of Scripture)— and informed by the significance of *regula fidei* as understood by Seitz, Treier, and Green—that I would like to propose a reading of Genesis 38 in the Christian context. The preceding sections in this book have demonstrated that the story of Judah and Tamar is integral to the patriarchal narratives with respect to the transmission of God's promise to Abraham. As developed previously, chapter 38 as a unit is primarily concerned with the inheritance of the portion of kingship in the triadic promise— effected in Abraham and his descendants through the birthright, the right of the firstborn.

A ruled reading in the transmission of kingship In the sense of *regula fidei* as prescribed above, the transmission of kingship in the patriarchal narrative should be seen as the

---

16. Ibid., 73–74.

pre-incarnational move of God in Christ to recover and reconcile man back to God's original intention in creation that man may rule and reign as His regent on the earth (Gen. 1:26–28). In this respect, the rule of faith dictates that this line of God's economy in the reconciliation and recovery of man—if indeed it is the subject of *tota Scriptura*—should be discernable across both Testaments of Christian Scripture. We will develop this thought in the next section of the book—Part 4: Destiny of Kingship.

Section summary A Christian reading of the story of Judah and Tamar in Genesis 38 must be modeled after the examples set by Jesus and His apostles. It is a Christ-centered reading that assumes the incarnation, death and resurrection of the second of the Divine Trinity as the subject of both testaments of Scripture. To this end, the God of Abraham, Isaac and Jacob superintended both Scripture and community to bear witness to His intention in Christ. The rise of modern historical criticism with its "scientific" criteria in judging what goes into the final form of biblical text have called into question this unified purpose of Scripture: bearing witness to Christ as well as forming and shaping the community of faith—Israel in the Old Testament, and the church in the New.

The canonical approach that Childs pioneered is a radical text-immanent interpretation of the Old Testament that places emphasis on the final form of Scripture as canonical. This is a critical step if we are to recover an interpretation of the first Testament that does justice to the examples set by Jesus and His apostles. While Childs' agenda is not about returning Old Testament interpretation to a pre-critical era in biblical scholarship—his coupling of the function of the canon of Scripture with the community of faith merits attention. In God's intention in Christ across both Testaments, Scripture and community are inseparable. God superintended the Israel of Old as a community to bear witness to the One who has as yet to come in the first Testament; and He continued with the new community of faith through the writings of the apostles in the second Testament—that the church may reach the goal that God intended for her.

Thus the second Testament was written by the apostles in step with a model of interpretation exemplified by Jesus, and this practice is continued in the ministry of the Spirit of truth—with the tacit assumption that the artifacts of the first Testament are records concerning Christ's pre-incarnated activities. While the Old Testament needs to be read in its own formal integrity, a Christian reading of the first Testament applies the *rule of faith* in order to grasp the order and larger coherence of Scripture as centering on the hidden life of Christ in the Old, and His explicit manifestation in the New Testament. Our reading of the story of Judah and Tamar must follow suit in tracing this pattern of God's action in Christ in His pre-incarnation, and its continuing narrative in the incarnated Christ across both Testaments of Christian Scripture.

Part 4: Destiny of Kingship

Overview

Part 4 models a ruled reading of Genesis 38 for the destiny of believers. Having read the story of Judah and Tamar in a second millennium BC historical context in Part 2, and armed with the rule of faith for traversing to the present in Part 3—we are now in a position to explore the meaning of kingship for New Testament believers. This entails an understanding of the inheritance of the kingship portion of the birthright in Christ's pre-incarnated and incarnated move. The canonicity of such a reading can be authenticated from the witness that Christian Scripture gives to the story of Judah and Tamar in its entirety. Such a reading parallels the teaching of the New Testament on grace and responsibility with respect the believers' inheritance of kingship as the right of the church of the firstborn.

Section Outline

Part 4: Destiny of Kingship

Section Introduction

17. The Triune pattern of God's operation
- o God's recovery from generation to generation
- o Unbroken witness of God's work

18. The kingship in Christ's pre-incarnated move
- o Judah—his transformation for kingship
- o A shadow of Him who is to come
- o Endorsement of the canon of Scripture

19. The kingship in Christ's incarnated move
- o Saved into the kingdom
- o The kingdom in development

20. Scripture's testimony to the theme of kingship

21. A Christian reflection on the story of Judah and Tamar
- o Christian heritage and responsibility as the church of the firstborn
- o The gospel of the grace of God and of Christ
- o The gospel of the kingdom
- o Ministry of reconciliation for the kingdom

Section Summary

Destiny of Kingship

Section Introduction

Taking our cue from the church fathers, a Christian reading of the story of Judah and Tamar should be based on the *hypothesis* of Scripture, by identifying a *pattern* in the order, arrangement, or connection of the Triune God's operation and move across both Testaments. Such a pattern is clearly discernable in *God's operation of reconciliation* to recover fallen mankind back to their birthright of kingship as ordained by God in creation. Genesis 1:28 sets in motion the unchanging motif of kingship in God's eternal intention for humankind created in His image and likeness, "... Be fruitful and multiply and fill the earth and *subdue* it and have *dominion* over the fish of the sea and over the birds of the heavens and over every living thing that moves on the earth [*emphasis added in italics*]."

The charge to subdue the earth and have dominion over the realms of the air, the sea and the earth is clearly a command to rule over creation on God's behalf. What is first recorded here at the dawn of creation will subsequently inform the structure and substance of the rest of Genesis, the Pentateuch (the Five Books of Moses), the Prophets, the Writings, and onwards through the New Testament to its consummation in Revelation. Thus what is ordained at the outset of Adam and Eve's creation is an unchanging line of God's eternal intention—that mankind has a divinely appointed destiny to rule and reign as God's regent.

17. The Triune pattern of God's operation

Sufficient weight must of necessity be given to this pattern of God's operation, if we are to grasp the significance of the recovery of the kingship portion of Abraham's promise in the story of Judah and Tamar. When seen in this light, the Fall in Genesis 3 is a major division marker in the destiny of mankind that cannot be ignored. As the chart in Appendix D below illustrates, there is a discernable pattern in the narrative structure of God's recovery of mankind from generation to generation in the Book of Genesis.

APPENDIX D

Narrative Structure of God's Recovery from Generation to Generation

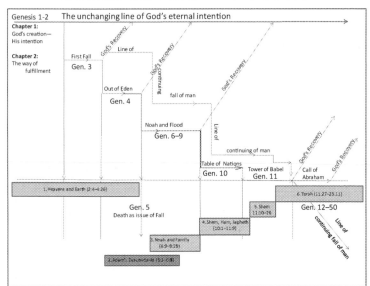

God's recovery from generation to generation Events that transpired before the Fall (chapters 1–2) speaks of God's eternal intention while the creation was still in pristine condition. Events thereafter are distorted by sin due to the Fall. On one side of the dividing line of Genesis 3, we have the revelation of God's eternal plan for mankind. Over against this unchanging line of God's intention, Genesis records a series of downward steps depicting mankind's continuous departure from the unchanging line of God's purpose. Mankind descended from the first Fall in Eden (Chap. 3) to the first murder (Chap. 4), to wholesale evil and wickedness (Chap. 6), to uttermost rebellion against God (Chap. 11). God's counter plan to bring mankind back to His intention immediately follows that of each step of humanity's descend—beginning with the promise of the seed of the woman in Genesis 3:15, who in time would bruise the head of the serpent.

Unbroken witness of God's work Indeed, as the following chart in Appendix E shows, there is an unbroken line to God's recovery and witness through the generations. It runs from Adam to Abel, Seth, Enosh, Enoch and Noah; then Shem, Terah and Abraham. But due to mankind's wholesale rejection of God in the rebellion at the Tower of Babel, the focus of God's saving operation to reconcile fallen man turned to Abraham and his line (Gen. 12). Henceforth, the promise of the seed of the woman would find continuity in the promise of the seed that would come through God's dealings with Abraham, Isaac and Jacob. In so doing, God established a pattern of operation in concord with Himself as the God of Abraham, Isaac, and Jacob (Exod. 3:16)— thus foreshadowing in these three specific men the nature of His move as triadic, conforming to His Triune existence and identity.

APPENDIX E

Unbroken Line of God's Recovery and Witness versus Man's Fall

Prologue (1:1–2:3)	Heavens and Earth (2:4–4:26)	Adam's Descendants (5:1–6:8)	Noah and Family (6:9–9:29)	Shem, Ham, Japheth (10:1–11:9)	Shem (11:10–26)	Terah (11:27–25:11)
God's Creation (1:1–2:25)						Abraham (11:26–25:11)
God's Creation—His intention	Man's Fall Issuing in Death (3:1–5:32)					
The way of fulfillment	Eden—Adam's Fall			Escalation of Man's Fall (6:1–11:9)		Terah (11:24–32)
	Out of Eden—Cain's' Fall		Fall of Noah's generation	Tower of Babel		
				Shem (6:10–11:26)		
			Noah (5:29–9:29)			
		✓ Enoch (5:22–24)				
	✓ Enosh: Men call on Lord 4:26)					
	✓ Seth (4:25–6:8)					
	✓ Abel (4:2–9)					
	✓ Adam (3:6–5.5)					

In the narrative of Genesis, we see an imprint of who God is that would be visible across the two testaments of Christian Scripture (Matt. 22:32, 28:19; Mark 12:26; Luke 20:37). The patriarchal narrative is the story of the Triune God (Treier) in action for man's reconciliation. It was through His Triune operations upon these three men—Abraham, in his calling and justification (Gen. 12, 15); Isaac, in his "death" and return to Abraham in "resurrection" (Gen. 22, Heb. 11:17–19); and Jacob, in being dealt with for transformation and maturity (Gen. 25–50)—that the Triune God pursued a divine program of reconciliation to recover the man He created. In essence, to enter into the inheritance or birthright of Abraham, Isaac and Jacob is to enter into a divine reconciliation of the Trinity for mankind's recovery, that the created and fallen human race may arrive at God's intention for him through the triadic promise of the land, the priesthood, and the kingship.

18. The kingship in Christ's pre-incarnated move

So a canonical reading of the story of Judah and Tamar must be located within this paradigm of Christ's pre-incarnated activity for mankind's reconciliation and recovery. As we have seen, chapter 38 of Genesis is a unit that continues God's saving operation upon Jacob in his life story that extended from chapters 25 to 50. The result of what transpired in the story of Judah and Tamar is Judah's eventual inheritance of the kingship for the brothers' reconciliation, to coincide with Joseph's reign over Egypt for the preservation of the children of Israel. Both are aspects of God's dealings with Jacob for dominion, so that he and his descendants may rule according to God's intent. This is the Triune imprint that God had established in His creation of mankind for His intention ("Let *us* make man according to *our* image and likeness," and "let them rule ...").

God's untiring effort for the reconciliation and recovery of mankind started with Adam's fall ("Where are you?") and is portrayed in toledot schema in subsequent generations of Adam, Noah, Noah's sons, and Shem (the first eleven chapters of Genesis). The pattern of God's Triune operation in His continuing work on Terah's descendants Abraham, Isaac, and Jacob (from the latter half of Genesis 11 onwards) should and must be brought to bear in reading Genesis 38. From this perspective, the eyes of faith sees a pre-incarnated Christ in His move to reconcile a fallen Judah to Himself, effected through Tamar's seeking of the birthright, the right of her husband as the firstborn according to God's ordination. Through two aspects of the birthright—God's sovereignty and man's responsibility—Tamar became the agency for God's turnaround of Judah's situation in Adullam. Thus the human crisis in the death of Judah's sons (initiated by God) became the searching, sweeping, and receiving operation[1] of the pre-incarnated Christ in His move among His elect in the ancient village of Adullam.

In the midst of Judah's alienation and failure, this move of the Trinity in the Son in seeking after him brought about an eventual reconciliation between Judah and Tamar (Gen. 38:26); Judah and his brothers—inclusive of Joseph (Gen. 42:21); and Judah and his father, Jacob (43:1–8; 44:1–34; 46:12, 28). Last but not least, it reunited the house of Jacob and reconciled Israel's situation with God and His intention for them. At the beginning of Genesis 38, the house of Jacob was scattered in three directions: Hebron, Adullam, and Egypt (Gen. 37:14, 36; 38:1). At the end of Genesis, we see a reunited and reconciled Israel in Egypt, ready for the next episode of the Son's pre-incarnated move in Exodus in the continuing saga of the Triune

---

1. In the order, connection, and coherence of Scripture, God's search for fallen man in Adam, Noah, Abraham, Isaac, Jacob, and now Judah unveils the Triune God's saving love toward the man He created for His purpose. This hypothesis of the Trinity in His move in the Son is made explicit in the three parables the Lord told in Luke 15 concerning: (1) a shepherd searching for a lost sheep, verses 1 to 7; (2) a woman sweeping for a lost coin, verses 8 to 10; and (3) a father receiving his lost son, verses 11 to 32. These parables graphically portray the Triune operation of God in seeking after sinners and reconciling them to the Father.

God's reconciliation and recovery of fallen man back to His intention. The repercussions of the story of Judah and Tamar in the patriarchal and Pentateuchal narratives (and more so when viewed from the perspective of the entire canon of Scripture[2]) is out of proportion with its literary placing as a single chapter in Genesis precisely because the God of Abraham, Isaac and Jacob intended it as such!

I thus submit that the impact of Genesis 38 across the millennia as seen in the order, connection, and arrangement of scriptural development in Judah's line is of God—and faith sees a hidden hand at work that cannot be explained by mere human motivation and actions, such as preserving the community as the sole intention of this story in the Bible. The account arises from God's operation in the pre-incarnated Son, in which He seeks, transforms, and reconciles Judah back to Himself. The kingship that Judah received is the issue of God's work upon him, for to inherit this aspect of the promise of the God of his fathers is to enter into the same saving operation of God that Abraham, Isaac, and Jacob experienced.

This then is the significance of Judah's blessing!

He entered into the saving work of the God of Abraham, Isaac and Jacob, a work carried out upon him that would in time make him who God wants him to be.

---

2. See the discussion in *Part 2*, section 11 above, *Birthright: key to the story of Judah and Tamar.*

Judah—his transformation for kingship How do we relate Judah's experience in the recovery of kingship in Genesis 38 to the canon of Scripture? There are many aspects of the kingdom that are covered in Scripture: God's governance, sovereignty, ruling, and our responsibility, discipline, discipleship, rights of citizenship, blessing or reward, punishment, and so on. But I would like to draw attention to one aspect that is prominent in the Scripture's commendation of Judah. 1 Chronicles says that Judah inherited the kingship because he prevailed over his brothers (1 Chron. 5:2a NASB).[3]

Unfortunately the New International Version (NIV) of the Bible has rendered this as "Judah was the 'strongest' of his brothers and a ruler came from him ..." It seems to me, the word *strongest* here is rather vague. Does it mean he lorded it over them? Did he rule over his brothers? Or defeat them in some way, beat them down, overpower them? What is the right connotation for *strong* or *prevail* in the context of Judah's inheritance of the kingship?

The Hebrew word here is *gabar*, the verbal form of which appears twenty-six times in the Old Testament. It has been variously translated as *rose* (Gen. 7:18), *great* (Ps. 117:2), *strong* (2 Sam. 1:23), *prevail* (1 Sam. 2:9), *overpower* (2 Sam. 11:23), *overwhelm* (Ps. 65:3), *arrogant* (Job 36:9), *triumph* (Isa. 42:13), *confirm* (Dan. 9:27), and so on. Gesenius gives the meaning as strong or prevail, but the primary power described here is that of

---

3. The English Standard Version (ESV) reads "Judah became strong among his brothers."

binding—to *bind up anything broken, to make firm.*[4] Harris, Archer, and Waltke added that in cognate Arabic, the basic meaning of the root is *to rise, raise, restore.*[5] Given the possible semantic range of *gabar*, how do we understand it when Scripture says that Judah *prevailed* over his brothers?

A shadow of Him who is to come The person that Judah became in God's saving operation that fitted him for the inheritance of the kingship was God's doing. It was the saving operation of the God of Abraham, Isaac, and Jacob that transformed him in figure into the likeness of the firstborn Son of God. In Judah's eventual role in Genesis, we see in silhouette aspects of what Jesus would be in the gospels: One who prevailed over, or *rose above*, every negative condition in His time to serve His disciples, followers, and fallen mankind for their reconciliation to God. Indeed, as Jesus replied when the mother of the two sons of Zebedee came to petition for them to be seated at His right and left hand in the kingdom, "Whoever would be great among you must be your servant, and whoever would be first among you must be your slave, even as the Son of Man came not to be served but to serve, and to give his life as a ransom for many" (Matt. 20:26–28).

This in shadow is what Judah became, so he could serve his brothers and the house of Jacob in the reconciliation. And the

---

4. S. P. Tragelles, trans., *Gesenius' Hebrew-Chaldee Lexicon of the Old Testament: Numerically Coded to Strong's Exhaustive Concordance* (Grand Rapids: Baker, 1979), 155.

5. R. L. Harris, G. L. Archer Jr., and B. K. Waltke, *Theological Wordbook of the Old Testament: Vol. I, Aleph to Mem* (Chicago: Moody Press, 1980), 148.

proper connotation for *gabar* in Judah's conduct and action after he was recovered suggests itself. We see him confessing his wrongs against Tamar and Joseph (Gen. 38:26, 42:21). He offered himself as surety for Benjamin to his father Jacob and again as a slave to Joseph for Benjamin to be released (43:1–8; 44:1–34; 46:12, 28). Judah's tenderheartedness for his father comes across when he appealed poignantly to Joseph, "No. Do not let me see the misery that would come upon my father" (44:34 NIV).[6] These tender sentiments on Judah's part is the outcome of God's work on him, and because of this he was entrusted with leadership (46:28) over his brothers for the purpose of serving them, and not, as it were, lording it over his brethren in any show of outward strength.

Instead he prevailed (*gabar*) over his brothers. He *rose above* every contrary situation that existed in Jacob's family to "contend" on behalf of his brethren in order to *mend that which was broken*, *bind them together*—so the house of Jacob, which was broken up, could be *restored*, *made whole* again, and *reconciled* to God. This confirmed God's selection of the house of Jacob, not in their own merit but in the grace of the God of Abraham, Isaac, and Jacob. Moses echoed this when he blessed the sons of Israel: "And this regarding Judah; so he said, 'Hear, O LORD, the voice of Judah, And bring him to his people. With his hands he contended for them, And may You be a help against his adversaries'" (Deut. 33:7 NASB).

6. ESV reads "I fear to see the evil that would find my father."

Not only was Judah contending for his brothers, but in his contending, God was also contending for him. Mere human words, such as "a change in character," fall far short in describing the qualities necessary for such a service. I venture that in light of Christ's pre-incarnated activity; prevailing over his brothers required an intrinsic work on Judah that foreshadowed what would later be revealed as the destiny of the chosen in the second Testament, "For those whom he foreknew he also predestined to be conformed to the image of his Son, in order that he might be the firstborn among many brothers" (Rom. 8:29).

Endorsement of the canon of Scripture In the course of time, the community of faith would come to recognize this imprint of God's work in their resounding endorsement of Judah (and Tamar) in the canon of *tota Scriptura* (Gen. 49:8–12; Deut. 33:7; Ruth 4:12–13; 1 Chron. 2:4, 5:1; Ezek. 47:13; Matt. 1:1–3; Rev. 5:5). Scripture's commendation of Judah and Tamar is an endorsement of God's work and a statement of divine priority in the affairs of man. Through this, the canon shaped the perception and attitude of God's people, and in turn the community of the faithful would come to recognize and value those who sought after God in like manner—such as Ruth (and Boaz) during the chaotic times of the Judges. Indeed, as Childs observed, the canon shaped the community of faith and vice versa. For the canon is the witness of a people who heard God's voice and recognized His footsteps and so arrayed their perception, values, life, and faith to be in step with the very God who first gave it being and voice—*it* referring to both the canon and the community (John 10:27) as subsisting in and mutually informed by the God of Abraham, Isaac and Jacob who gives life to the dead and calls the things not being as being (Rom. 4:17).

This proposed reading recognizes God's pre-incarnated activity that carries forward into the second Testament, in the Son's incarnated move for man's reconciliation for kingship. In time, the second Testament would recognize this voice and footprint in the first and so would begin the New Testament age with the trumpeting of "The book of the genealogy [generation] of Jesus Christ, the son of David, the son of Abraham. *Abraham* was the father of *Isaac*, and Isaac the father of *Jacob*, and Jacob the father of *Judah* and his brothers, and Judah the father of *Perez* and Zerah by *Tamar* ... and Jacob the father of Joseph the husband of Mary, by whom was born Jesus, who is called *Christ (emphasis added in italics)*" (Matt. 1:1–3, 16).

All the key people under God's saving operation in the patriarchal narratives and, within that, the story of Genesis 38 (summarized as *Judah and his brothers, and Judah the father of Perez and Zerah by Tamar*), appear prominently in the generations that brought forth Jesus Christ. Judah is mentioned immediately after Jacob, ahead of his brothers, "Judah and his brothers ..." (Matt. 1:2). In this way, the Triune God endorsed His operation in Judah and Tamar, as God's move in His pre-incarnated Son—Christ—in Genesis 38 as part of the patriarchal narrative. And so the story of Judah and Tamar within the realm of God's triadic operation as the God of Abraham, Isaac, and Jacob finds its validity across the millennia in the incarnation of the Son.

19. The kingship in Christ's incarnated move

With the birth of Judah's great progeny, Jesus Christ, the story of the Triune God in effecting man's recovery for the kingship continues in the ministry of reconciliation of the incarnated Son. The first verse of the second Testament begins with king Jesus, the Son of David, and therefore the rightful heir to the throne (Matt. 1:1; 2 Sam 7:12–14). This Jesus, the seed of the kingdom, is Jehovah our Savior (Matt. 1:21). To believe in Jesus as Savior (1:1–2, 21) is to believe in the God of Abraham, Isaac and Jacob, and in so doing, enter into the same heritage of the patriarchs. All three aspects of Abraham's promise find their fulfillment in Jesus Christ, as the One in whom all Scripture is directed.[7] So to enter into this heritage is to enter into God's saving work in the Son in His incarnation, death and resurrection for man's reconciliation to God, and be brought into the inheritance of kingship in the line of Judah reflecting God's intention that man would rule and have dominion in Him.

---

7. The physical land allotted to the Israelites was the realm upon which they conducted their living and labored for their livelihood. The land thus typifies Christ as the share of the allotted portion of the saints in the light (Col. 1:12). Analogically, even as the land was the Israelite's allotted portion, today Christ is our portion, and as such He is the realm in which we have been put as a new creation through baptism (Rom. 6:3–4; 2 Cor. 5:17), and in Him we walk, having been rooted and grounded in faith (Col. 2:6–7). Consequently, we are to gain Christ (Phil. 3:8) and labor in Him in power (Col. 1:29)—even as the Israelites had to gain the land and labor on it, not only that they may have a livelihood but also that they would have something to bring to God in worship. This is not to say that the promise concerning the land has no physical fulfillment today (undeniably there is this aspect—see Matt. 5:5; Rom. 4:13; Heb. 2:5–8); only that its greater significance is Christ. And with regard to the priesthood and the kingship, the New Testament obviously finds their ultimate realization in the person of Christ (Heb. 8:1–2; 4:14–15; 7:25–26; Matt. 2:2, 21:5, 27:11; John 12:13; Rev. 15:3, 17:14, 19:16).

Saved into the kingdom   Thus to be saved is to be saved into the kingdom of God. The first words of Jesus' ministry concerned the kingdom (Matt. 4:17, Mark 1:15). And so the program of God's salvation is also a program of recovery of the blessing of kingship for the kingdom[8] that God promised Abraham. This was first intended for the house of Jacob (John 4:22), but they would miss it due to their hardheartedness in rejecting their King in His first advent (Matt. 23:37–38). In this One, as Isaiah once prophesied, the Gentiles would place their hope ahead of the house of Jacob (Matt. 12:17–18, 21; Rom. 15:12; Isa. 11:10, 42:4, 61:1). Henceforth, the Son's work of reconciliation for the recovery of the kingdom would reach out to the Gentiles (Matt. 8:10–12, 28:19–20), fulfilling God's promise to Abraham that he would be a blessing to all nations.

The kingdom in development   In the developing story of the New Testament, we see the enlargement of God's reconciling work for the kingdom, from the calling of the first group of disciples Andrew, Peter, James, and John (Matt. 4:18–22), to the twelve and seventy (Matt. 10:1; Luke 10:1), and then the hundred and twenty praying in one accord in the upper room (Acts 1:14–15). The hundred and twenty were charged to

---

8. The many occurrences of the word *kingdom* throughout the Gospels makes this more than obvious: Matt. 3:2; 4:17, 23; 5:3, 10, 19f; 6:10, 33; 7:21; 8:11f; 9:35; 10:7; 11:11f; 12:25f, 28; 13:11, 19, 24, 31, 33, 38, 41, 43ff, 47, 52; 16:19, 28; 18:1, 3f, 23; 19:12, 14, 23f; 20:1, 21; 21:31, 43; 22:2; 23:13; 24:7, 14; 25:1, 34; 26:29; Mark 1:15; 3:24; 4:11, 26, 30; 6:23; 9:1, 47; 10:14f, 23ff; 11:10; 12:34; 13:8; 14:25; 15:43; Luke 1:33; 4:43; 6:20; 7:28; 8:1, 10; 9:2, 11, 27, 60, 62; 10:9, 11; 11:2, 17f, 20; 12:31f; 13:18, 20, 28f; 14:15; 16:16; 17:20f; 18:16f, 24f, 29; 19:11f, 15; 21:10, 31; 22:16, 18, 29f; 23:42, 51; John 3:3, 5; 18:36. This theme would continue with Acts, into the epistles, and consummate in Revelation with the kingdom of this world becoming the kingdom of our Lord and of His Christ; and that He shall reign forever and ever (Rev. 11:15).

tarry in Jerusalem until the promise of the Father came upon them (Luke 24:45; Acts 1:5). The promise of the Father was part of God's unifying plan,[9] which started with the promise of the seed of the woman in Genesis 3:15 and was later developed in the promise given to Abraham (Gen. 12:1–3). It refers to the blessing of Abraham that would come to the Gentiles through Jesus Christ so they might receive the promise of the Spirit through faith (Gal. 3:14).

The Lord spoke about this promise in Luke 24:49 when He said, "And behold, I am sending the promise of My Father upon you. But stay in the city until you are clothed with power from on high." Luke takes up the subject again in Acts 1:5 by reminding readers that "John baptized with water, but you will be baptized with the Holy Spirit not many days from now." Then in Acts 2:14–21, the apostle Peter in his first message to the Jews explained that the outpouring of the Holy Spirit was promised by God in Joel. The context in Acts 1 in which the baptism of the Holy Spirit was introduced is the Lord's forty-day discourse concerning the kingdom of God (Acts 1:3–5, 8).

With the baptism of the Holy Spirit—first of the Jews (Acts 2) and then the Gentiles at the house of Cornellius (Acts 10)—the church, the body of Christ as the kingdom of God, would come into being (1 Cor. 12:13) as the new community of faith. From a hundred and twenty in the upper room, three thousand would be baptized at Pentecost in response to Peter's preaching on the resurrected

9. W. C. Kaiser Jr. "The Spirit Baptism in the Holy Spirit as the Promise of the Father: A Reformed Perspective," *Perspectives on Spirit Baptism*, ed. by C. O. Brand (Nashville: B&H, 2004), 16–19.

Christ (Acts 2:41). Eventually many more (Gk. *myriads*, or ten thousand) in Jerusalem would be added (21:20). A close study of the contents of the entire book of Acts reveals that the baptism of the Holy Spirit inaugurated the spreading of the gospel of the kingdom of the resurrected and ascended Christ by the Spirit. This was accomplished through the disciples to produce the churches as the kingdom of God, starting from Jerusalem, through Judea and Samaria, to the uttermost parts of the earth. The recovery of kingship that began with Judah in Genesis 38 would ripple across the millennia and eventually reach the farthest shore, in the preaching of the gospel of the kingdom to the whole inhabited earth (Matt. 24:14).

20. Scripture's testimony to the theme of kingship

It seems to me that such a reading is worthy of the prominence Scripture has accorded the line of Judah in the kingship, and it pertains to the greatness of the God of Abraham, Isaac and Jacob who made it such. Contrary to the opinions of certain scholars, Scripture unequivocally assigns Genesis 38 a critical part in the story of the Triune God in His move across both Testaments. The reconciling work that God began in His recovery of Judah would reverberate through the centuries over the two Testaments from Genesis to Revelation, in the canon of Christian Scripture. The theme of recovery of kingship through Judah and its continuation in his line would see an impressive development from generation to generation throughout the entire Bible:[10]

- From the recovery of Judah in Genesis 38 through the agency of Tamar,

- To his role in the reconciliation of the house of Jacob (Gen. 43:1–8, 44:1–34, 46:12, 28)

- To Jacob's prophecies that the scepter would not depart from Judah in Genesis 49 (Gen. 1:26–28, 49:10),

- To the position of Judah as the leading tribe in the east in Israel's encampment, march, and fighting as an army through the wilderness in Numbers (Num. 2:1-3),

- To Moses' blessing of Judah in Deuteronomy as Judah contended for his people, with the Lord at his side against his adversaries (Deut. 33:7),

- To the leadership of Joshua (tribe of Ephraim) and Caleb (tribe of Judah) in the conquest of the good land (Num. 13:6),

- To its fulfillment in David who was firstly king of Judah, and then overall king of Israel (2 Sam. 2–5, 8, 10; 1 Chron. 11:1-9; 18:1–19:19),

10. Gen. 1:26–28, 49:10; Deut. 33:7; Num. 2:1–3, 13:6, 14:6, 24, 30; 1 Sam. 13:14, 16:10–13; 2 Sam. 7:12b, 12:24; Jer. 23:5; Matt. 1:6; 1 Chron. 3:1, 10, 17, 19; Ezra 5:1, 2; Zech. 4:7–10; Matt. 1:1, 23; Isa. 7:14; Gal. 4:4; Luke 3:23, 38; Rev. 5:5, 10; 11:15; 20:4–6; 22:16.

- To Solomon, the son of David, who built the temple at the height of Israel in the period of monarchy (2 Sam. 7; 1 Chron. 17, 22, 28, 29),

- To Zerubbabel, the head of the tribe of Judah in his leadership role in the exile's return from Babylonian captivity and the rebuilding of God's temple (Haggai 1:1; Matt. 1:6, 12),

- To Jesus' birth as the Son of David, Son of Abraham, and Son of Adam—thus fulfilling God's promise concerning the seed of the woman and the seed of Abraham (Gen. 3:15; Matt. 1:1, 16), and

- To its consummation in the book of Revelation, in the kingship's ultimate realization in Jesus Christ as the King of kings; in His coming again in the second advent to establish His eternal reign as the *Lion of the tribe of Judah* over a kingdom enlarged to fill the whole earth (Rev. 5:5, 10; 11:15; 20:4–6; 22:16).

And so, when the New Testament opens, the Triune God has journeyed through forty-two generations of people associated with Him (as filtered through the genealogical lens of Matthew chapter 1) to fulfill in Jesus Christ—as a descendant of David and Abraham, and through the line of Judah—God's intention from the beginning that man created in His image and likeness would rule and reign as God's regent on the earth. With Christ's ministry in the second Testament, what was promised to Abraham—that kings would come from his loin—is fully realized, and as Jacob once prophesied so long ago, "The scepter shall not depart from Judah, nor the ruler's staff from between his feet, until the tribute comes to him; and to him shall be the obedience of the peoples" (Gen. 49:10).

Amen!

21. A Christian reflection on the story of Judah and Tamar

Goldingay bemoans the disarray in doctrinal understanding of Scripture.[11] A reason he advanced is the nature of the models used for theological thinking that for the most parts do not derive from Scripture. In his opinion, even the models for theological reflection must be made in the light of Scripture. The contextual theological reflection in the Romans and Corinthian letters are good examples to emulate. The illumination that Paul received for addressing situational issues in the church resulted from pouring over Scriptures in the context of the gospel.

In 1 Corinthians, the apostle takes up a series of issues in the Corinthian church life when he wrote to the believers in that city. In Goldingay's words, Paul's writings are the "... fruit of reflection on these [that is, the Corinthian issues] in light of a Christian understanding of creation, the story of Israel, the incarnation, the

---

11. J. Goldingay, *Key Questions about Biblical Interpretation: Old Testament Answers* (Grand Rapids: Baker Academic, 2011), 138–142.

cross, the resurrection, and the future appearing of Jesus."[12] This example on Christian reflection can also be seen in the Epistle to the Romans. In chapters 9–11, the apostle considered the question of Israel's failure to recognize Jesus as Messiah in light of the first Testament so he could give a satisfactory theological account of it in the face of God's promise and faithfulness. According to Goldingay, these two instances model an analytical, discursive process for Christian thinking that looks at pressing situational issues in the light of the first Testament and the gospel of Jesus Christ.

Christian heritage and responsibility as the church of the firstborn The story of Judah and Tamar offers an opportunity for similar contextual theological reflection today with regard to our Christian heritage and responsibility as the church of the firstborn (Heb. 12:23). We Christians, born of God, are the firstfruits of God's creatures (James 1:18) that He reaped in His creation. In that sense we are the firstborn sons of God. Hence the church, composed of us, is called the church of the firstborn. As the firstborn sons of God, we have the birthright. This includes the inheritance of the earth (James 2:5–6; Matt. 5:5; Rom. 4:13, 16), the priesthood (Rev. 20:6), and the kingship (Rev. 20:4).

As we have seen in the preceding sections, the dynamics of the inheritance of the birthright in the patriarchal narratives has a dual aspect: God's sovereignty and ordination, as well as man's responsibility and coordination. Echoing this, the Epistle to the

---

12. Ibid., 139.

Hebrews, after five progressive warnings,[13] makes particular reference to the lesson of Esau vis-à-vis the birthright in these stern words: "See to it that no one fails to obtain the grace of God; that no root of bitterness springs up and causes trouble, and by it many be defiled; that no one is sexually immoral or unholy like Esau, who sold his own birthright for a single meal. For you know that afterward, when he desired to inherit the blessing, he was rejected, for you know that afterward, he found no chance to repent, though he sought it with tears (Heb. 12:15–17)." This is a sobering word with regard to our Christian heritage (a matter of God's ordination) and our responsibility (a question of our obedience and cooperation) as the church of the firstborn.

The church today, existing as it were in a post-modern, permissive age with relative morals and values, needs to exercise vigilance in its instruction of believers. All too often there is a risk of looseness when it comes to our Christian sense of responsibility, outlook, and propriety concerning the things of God and ourselves, and His intention for the kingdom. While it is true that today's post-modern culture is a contributing factor, perhaps a reason closer to home is a lack of proper understanding concerning "grace" in the New Testament.

---

13. The epistle to the Hebrews was written to certain believers who were in danger of falling from grace and returning to Judaism. So the writer presented the superiority of Christ and the Christian's heritage in the New Covenant and admonished the Hebrew believers to press on, with these warnings: (1) give heed to what is spoken concerning the Son, 2:1–4; (2) do not come short of the promised rest, 3:7–4:13; (3) be brought on to maturity, 5:11–6:20; (4) come forward to the Holy of Holies and do not shrink back, 10:19–39; and (5) run the race and do not fall away from grace,12:1–29.

It certainly is the teaching of Scripture that Christians are saved by faith alone, and are no longer under law but under grace (Rom. 6:14–15). However, it is possible that an inadequate realization of the richness of grace in the New Testament—in experience or instruction (or both) in Christian communities—leads indirectly to license for looseness and sinning in all sorts of ways (6:1). Potentially, this can be exacerbated by the prevailing though unbalanced view that we are saved by grace, and therefore, everything will be all right no matter what. Yet the Epistle to the Hebrews, with its five progressive warnings, should at least cause us to pause and ask if there may be something amiss that needs addressing.

Lest I am misunderstood, I confess wholeheartedly to assurance of salvation; that it is eternal and that once we are saved we will not perish eternally (John 10:28–29). Having so affirmed, this pressing question yet remains: if there is no sense in which a Christian would suffer some loss if he falls short of the grace of God, why these stern warnings in Hebrews with respect our Christian birthright? It is altogether inadequate exegesis to take these warnings on the possibility of coming short of the grace of God, as merely situational and applicable only to the Hebrews or to false Christians. As genuine Christians, we should and must reckon with it and take these warning messages seriously.

The gospel of the grace of God and of Christ The New Testament reveals the gospel of the grace of God, and the gospel of the grace of Christ (Acts 20:24, Gal. 1:6). The apostle Paul wrote clearly that justification is by grace through faith. It is the gift of God's grace through redemption in Christ (Rom. 3:24), and no one will be justified in God's sight through the works of the law (v. 20a). The law in the first Testament gave man the knowledge of sin (v. 20b), but it was weak because of man's flesh (8:3a). The entire economy of the first Testament in the law testifies to the fact that all have sinned and come short of the glory of God (3:23). In this sense, the economy of the law is inferior in that it makes demand of sinners, but it could not give life to enable fallen man to meet its requirements (Gal. 3:21).

The nature of the law is such that it could only make demands. There is nothing in the law that can enable fallen man to meet its requirements. The law can make the demand "You shall not gamble", but it cannot give man a "non gambling life" so that the doers of the law automatically fulfill the demand not to gamble. In this respect, the apostle Paul tells us that what the law could not do, God did by first sending His Son in the likeness of the flesh of sin that He might condemn sin in the flesh (Rom. 8:3b). But Paul did not just say this. He also tells us that "... the law of the Spirit of life has set you free in Christ Jesus from the law of sin and death" (v. 2). The "law of the Spirit of life" derives its veracity from the enabling divine life that God imparted into believers as the Spirit of life.

When someone believes in Jesus, their human spirit is born of the Spirit of God, for that which is born of the Spirit is spirit (John 3:6b). And so now, in the mystery of the economy of salvation in the second Testament, the righteousness of God has been manifested, apart from the law, and witnessed by the law and the prophets (Rom. 3:21). What God has accomplished in Christ fully meets the requirements of the law and the prophets. This is the righteousness of God through faith in Jesus Christ, for all who believe that the requirements of the law might be fulfilled in us who do not walk according to the law but according to the Spirit (3:21–22; 8:3). But the effective, experiential key to this grace we have received is contingent upon our obedience and actions.

We are to walk according to the Spirit and not according to the flesh (v. 4); by setting our minds on the things of the Spirit so our being may be according to the Spirit (vv. 5–6). This is to be our responsibility. If we cooperate with His indwelling operation; the enabling life of the Spirit will enliven our human spirit, mind, and even body through the Spirit who indwells us (vv. 6, 10–11). In this way, the indwelling Spirit (who is also the indwelling Christ, vv. 10–11) enables the Christian to fulfill the requirements of the law, through the life enablement of the Spirit of life who indwells their inner being.

This is the law of the Spirit of life overcoming the law of sin and death (v. 2) in our subjective experience of the gospel of the grace of God and Christ. In this and only this sense, Christ becomes the end of the law for righteousness to everyone who believes (10:4). Christ is the end of the outward law in that His very person in resurrection as the life-giving Spirit (1 Cor. 15:45a) is now our inward law. It does not mean that we can be loose, now that we are no longer under law but under grace. What it does mean is that God in Christ as the Spirit is now our indwelling law. The gift of the Spirit has been bestowed, and we have to cooperate with His inward leading, for as many as are led by the Spirit of God, these are the sons of God (Rom. 8:14). And only when the Spirit leads us are we not under law (Gal. 5:18) but under grace. The irony and balanced view of the second Testament is that when we are under grace—the inward demands of Christ, the demands of grace, are much higher than that of the New Testament (see Matt. 5:17–48).

According to the law and the prophets, it is sufficient not to murder, but the law of Christ says that "... everyone who is angry with his brother will be liable to judgment; whoever insults his brother will be liable to the council; and whoever says, 'You fool!' will be liable to the hell of fire" (Matt. 5:17, 22). Indeed, the section in Matthew on the uplifted law of the kingdom of heaven seals the law of Christ with "You therefore must be perfect, as your heavenly Father is perfect" (v. 48). But thanks be to God, for Romans 8 also reveals that with this highest demand in Christ, there is the highest supply through Him who indwells us if we cooperate with His leading within us.

Thus, we see that with the revelation of the gospel of grace, there is the same dual aspect that we first encountered in the transmission of the birthright in the patriarchal narrative. On the one hand, we Christians have been blessed with believing Abraham (Gal. 3:9), and in so believing, we have received the inheritance just like Abraham, Isaac, Jacob, and Judah (v. 16). In light of Paul's writings, God's promises to Abraham concerning the land (Rom. 4:13), the great nation (v. 17), and becoming a blessing to all nations (Gal. 3:8) are all promises made to Christ as the unique offspring of Abraham (not concerning many but one, v. 16). Actually, according to the apostle, Christ is both the singular heir and our unique inheritance (vv. 16, 29). As the One the promise was made to, He is the unique heir; as the singular seed of Abraham, He is our unique inheritance. What we have received in the New Testament is not at all a "thing", like the law in the Old Testament. What has come to us is a person, Christ Himself. Consequently, the apostle John could write, "For the law was given through Moses; grace and truth [or reality] came through Jesus Christ" (John 1:17).

Since we have been baptized into Christ, we are in Christ, whether Jew or Greek, and in Him we have become Abraham's seed, heirs according to promise (Gal. 3:27–29). And in Christ as the unique heir, we have received the inheritance, the blessing of Abraham; that is the *promise of the Spirit* by faith (v. 14). This Spirit, as the indwelling Spirit in all believers, is the blessing of Abraham! And we have received it not because of any merit of our own. It is of God that we are in Christ and not of ourselves. This speaks of God's sovereignty and ordination. And yet, having received the inheritance, we have a responsibility to cooperate with the Spirit who indwells us (Rom. 8:4–6, 13–14; 3:21–22; 6:12–16; Eph. 4:30), so we may partake in experience and enjoy the promise we have inherited. Otherwise, the grace given to us in the gospel would have been in vain (2 Cor. 6:1), and we would have fallen short of the grace of God (Heb. 12:15, Gal. 5:4).

The gospel of the kingdom We have seen in the first Testament, that the recovery of kingship in Judah would in the course of time lead to the anointing of David as king who reigned over Israel as subject (1 Sam. 1:13). The nation of Israel was the kingdom of God in the Old Testament. And the monarchy under David and Solomon was the high point of God's pre-incarnated activity in recovery and reconciliation of fallen man in the Old Testament. In the second Testament, the order and arrangement in the narration of God's incarnated move continues the theme of the kingdom. Matthew begins with the Baptist's preaching of the gospel of the kingdom (Matt. 3:1–2). And significantly, all four Gospels present the Spirit coming down upon Jesus before He began His ministry (Matt. 3:17; Mark 1:10; Luke 3:22; 4:18; John 1:32). That was the anointing of Jesus as king. Whereas the Old Testament kings were anointed with oil in figure, King Jesus was anointed with the Spirit in reality. Having been anointed, our King began His ministry with the words, "Repent, for the kingdom of heaven is at hand" (Matt. 4:17), and subsequently He went throughout Galilee to proclaim the gospel of the kingdom (v. 23).

When Jesus sent out the twelve apostles, He charged them to preach repentance for the kingdom to the lost sheep of the house of Israel (10:17). Near the end of His earthly ministry, He prophesied that the gospel of the kingdom would be preached to the whole inhabited earth, and then the end would come (24:14). In resurrection He appeared repeatedly to His disciples through a period of forty days to speak about the things concerning the kingdom (Acts 1:3). Then He charged them to wait in Jerusalem for the promise of the Father, for even as John baptized with water, they would be baptized with the Holy Spirit not many days hence (vv. 4–5). Thus, the baptism of the Holy Spirit is for the kingdom. With this baptism, the Head Christ shares His power and authority with His body for the preaching of the gospel of the kingdom and for the spreading of the churches from Jerusalem to Judea, Samaria, and the uttermost parts of the earth (Acts 5:11; 8:1, 3; 9:31; 11:22, 26; 12:1, 5; 13:1; 14:23, 27; 15:3f, 22; 18:22; 20:17, 28).

Clearly the second Testament preached to us the gospel of the kingdom. We were transferred into the kingdom (Col. 1:13) by being regenerated into the kingdom (John 3:5). Now we are in the kingdom (Rev. 1:9), which today is the proper Christian and church life in the Spirit (Rom. 14:17). On the one hand, as the church of the firstborn, the kingdom is our heritage. This speaks of God's ordination. On the other hand, it is also our responsibility. God's priority in His move across the two Testaments is the kingdom. His priority must become our priority.

If we follow Christ, we need to follow Him in the way of the kingdom (Matt. 16:18–19, 24–26). This is to render Him our cooperation. And so, we Christians have a responsibility to seek first the kingdom of God and His righteousness, and all the other things necessary for our earthly life and living will be added to us (6:33). God's move in and for the kingdom must permeate our consciousness, our being, and move so that the inner narratives of our deepest longing, seeking, and concern become patterned after the Lord's prayer concerning the kingdom. Pray then like this, He instructed: "Our Father in heaven, hallowed be your name. Your kingdom come, your will be done, on earth as it is in heaven. Give us this day our daily bread, and forgive us our debts as we also have forgiven our debtors. And lead us not into temptation, but deliver us from evil. *For Yours is the kingdom and the power and the glory forever. Amen* (emphasis added in italics)"[14] (Matt. 6:9–13).

Ministry of reconciliation for the kingdom   As kingdom people, Christians have a responsibility to walk in the footsteps of Jesus in our service to Him. Such a service is foreshadowed in Christ's pre-incarnated activities as revealed in Judah's role in Genesis. After Judah repented, he returned to be with his brothers and served them in the reconciliation of Jacob's family. God's pre-incarnated move in the Son, as seen through the story of Judah and Tamar, was for the reconciliation of the house of Jacob with a view to Israel as God's kingdom. In like manner, God's advancing move in the second Testament for man's reconciliation was first seen in the person of the Son and then through the ministry of His apostles. As is the case with Judah in the first Testament, God's kingdom in the second requires us to serve men in the way of reconciliation.

This is exemplified by the apostle Paul in his ministry to the Corinthian believers. According to Paul, God reconciled us to Himself through Christ so He could give to us the *ministry of reconciliation* (2 Cor. 5:18). In 2 Corinthians chapter 5, he indicated that man's full reconciliation to God is in two steps. First, God was

---

14. One manuscript has this as part of verse 13. So some translations, such as the New American Standard Version, carry this in italics, as part of its rendering of this verse.

in Christ for the expressed purpose of reconciling the world to Himself (v. 19). This is to reconcile sinners to God from sin. For this reason Christ died for our sins (1 Cor. 15:3) that we might be forgiven by God. Secondly, Christ died for us all so we would no longer live for ourselves but for Him who died and rose again on our behalf (v. 15). The problem with the Corinthian believers wasn't that they were not saved, but rather, having believed, they continued to live in themselves and for themselves—and not for God. The many references to the kingdom in the apostle's first letter to the Corinthians (4:20; 6:9, 10; 15:24, 50) inform us that the kingdom was Paul's main concern in dealing with the issues among them.

The Corinthian believers had experienced the first step of being reconciled to God as sinners, but a second step would be needed so they could live in the reality of the kingdom in the Spirit (Rom. 14:17; 1 Cor. 6:9–10, 17). Living in the reality of the kingdom requires believers to take up their cross daily (by the power of the indwelling Spirit) to deny their natural life in order that they may no longer live for themselves but for Christ who died for them. After the Lord revealed to Peter that He would build His church and that He would give to him the keys of the kingdom (Matt: 16:18–19), the Lord spoke to His disciples on the need to take up the cross daily, that they may experience the denial of their natural life (vv. 24–26). In other words, the denial of our natural life through taking up of the cross daily is the key to following Jesus in the pathway of the kingdom.

The many problems the Corinthians faced in their life and living in the church indicated that because they did not take up their cross to deny themselves, they were not living in the reality of the kingdom. The Lord was their king, but in reality they lived in themselves and for themselves. As a result they were divided (1 Cor. 1:10–17)—they sued each other over personal rights (6:1–11), they abused their freedom in Christ (6:12–20), they stumbled others in the matter of eating because the rich believers ate supper in a manner that did not care for the sensibilities of the poor members in the church (8:1–13); and the list of issues from their fallen natural life goes on and on. Consequently, the apostles labored among them as ambassadors of Christ—who had been committed with the word of reconciliation—to reconcile the Corinthian believers to each other and to God (2 Cor. 5:19–20) so they might become the righteousness of God in Christ (v. 21).

Paul's service to the church in Corinth is strongly reminiscent of Judah's service to the house of Jacob for the reconciliation of his brothers. This similarity is by no means coincidental but rather the *modus operandi* patented upon the God of Abraham, Isaac, and Jacob in reconciliation, first in His pre-incarnated activity in Judah and now through the apostle Paul for the Corinthian believers in the second Testament. That the apostle considered the many individual believers in Christ—the church, as the Israel of God (Gal. 6:16)—hints that Paul was consciously exercising the ministry of reconciliation entrusted to him over the church in Corinth as part of the spiritual house of Israel, even as Judah did for the house of Jacob in the first Testament.

Section summary This section presents a Christian reading of the story of Judah and Tamar in Scripture through the Christological lens of *regula fidei*, the rule of faith. It takes as authoritative the final form of the canon of Christian Scripture. Behind the rule of faith is the hypothesis of Scripture that there is a discernable pattern in the order, arrangement, or connection, of the Triune God's operation and move across both Testaments. This is clearly discernable in God's recovery of mankind after the Fall in Genesis 3. Following this pattern, a ruled reading of Genesis 38 sees Christ's pre-incarnated move in recovering a fallen Judah through Tamar's cooperation in her seeking after the birthright, the right of the firstborn. In so doing, God's ordination meets with man's responsibility in Tamar's cooperation and Judah's repentance. After Judah recovered, he prevailed over his brothers to serve them in the reconciliation of the house of Jacob. The canon of the first Testament, in its commendation of Judah and Tamar concerning the preservation of the kingship portion of the blessing of Abraham, recognized the saving operation of the God of Abraham, Isaac, and Jacob in the story recorded in Genesis 38.

Thus, from the perspective of the entire Bible, the story of Judah and Tamar is pivotal in the patriarchal narrative and throughout Scripture. What God began in the first Testament in recovering Judah for his inheritance of kingship would continue into the second Testament in the incarnation of the Son. With the birth of Judah's great progeny, Jesus Christ, the story of the Triune God in effecting mankind's recovery for kingship continues into the ministry of reconciliation of the incarnated Son. In Jesus as the seed of David and the seed of Abraham, God would fulfill His promise to Abraham concerning the land, the great nation (kingship), and becoming a blessing to all nations (priesthood). The blessing of Abraham would come to the Gentiles through Jesus Christ, that they might receive the promise of the Spirit through faith. When man received the Spirit, they would be regenerated and become part of the church as the kingdom of God (John 3:3, 5–6), the new Israel of God. In this way, the recovery of kingship that the God of Abraham, Isaac, and Jacob initiated in Judah in Genesis 38 would ripple across the two Testaments of Christian Scripture to eventually reach the whole inhabited earth through the preaching of the gospel of the kingdom.

This reading of the story of Judah and Tamar in a canonical context, based on the rule of faith, offers an opportunity for contextual theological reflection with respect to our Christian heritage and responsibility as the church of the firstborn (Heb. 12:23). The dual aspect of God's sovereignty and man's responsibility, first seen in the dynamic of the inheritance of the birthright, is attested to in the warnings recorded in the Epistle to the Hebrews. It is of God that we are in Christ, and in Christ we have received the blessing of the Spirit as the fulfillment of God's promise to Abraham. As such, we are no longer under law but under grace. This is God's ordination for us concerning our heritage as the church of the firstborn. But we do have a responsibility to live and walk according to the Spirit, for grace[15] to be operative in us. Otherwise the grace given to us would have been in vain.

Furthermore, in God's ordination and sovereignty, we have been saved into the kingdom. As such, the kingship is also our heritage. But just as Judah cooperated with God by exercising his "kingship" so he could prevail over his brothers for their reconciliation; as ambassadors of Christ, we also need to render our cooperation to God by entering into a ministry of reconciliation of two aspects in our service in the kingdom. First, we cooperate with Him to reconcile sinners to God. Second, we labor with Him to reconcile believers who are not living in the reality of the kingdom. This is to work with God for their growth in life (I planted and Apollos watered, but God gives the growth—1 Cor. 3:6)—through their perfecting that they may take up their cross daily to deny the outworking of their fallen natural life so that they may live no longer for themselves but for Him who died on their behalf. This is a two-step, God-ordained life procedure in our exercise of the ministry of reconciliation: bringing sinners to God and perfecting the believers in the church—the new house of Israel as the kingdom of God. It is what we render to God in obedient service,

---

15. The connotation of grace in this sense goes much deeper than just "unmerited favor." It is that for sure but also much more. Grace in its full import refers to our participation and experience of the Spirit as the blessing of Abraham that we received as our birthright when we believe in Jesus. According to the apostle Paul, the Spirit who indwells believers is the Spirit of life (Rom. 8:2, 6), the Spirit of God (v. 9a), the Spirit of Christ (v. 9b), Christ Himself (v.10), the Spirit of him who raised Jesus from the dead (v. 11). This is the full designation of the Spirit who is also the Spirit of sonship (vv. 14–17) in us, whose purpose it is to conform us to the image of Jesus as the firstborn Son of God in all His glory (vv. 14–17, 28–30). Such is the salvation of God in Christ that will make us the kingdom of God, and this is our birthright as believers in the church of the firstborn.

and by it He will exercise His saving power to fully reconcile the man He created for His intention; that they rule and reign on His behalf. This then is the life and service in the reality of the kingdom in the church today.

Part 5: Reigning in Life Today

Overview

Part 5 goes into the application of the story of Judah and Tamar in Genesis 38 for Christians. The kingship that Judah inherited foreshadows the ruling life of Christ in the church in resurrection. The church is to the new community of faith what the nation of Israel was to the kingdom of God in the Old Testament. Even as Tamar sought after the birthright, and Judah "prevailed" over his brothers to serve the house of Jacob for the realization of the kingdom in the first Testament; we need to seek the experience of Christ's kingly life that we may reign in His life in service to the church as God's kingdom today. Reigning in Christ's life is for our present experience in the church. It is a spiritual reality predicated upon the God of Abraham, Isaac and Jacob as the God of resurrection. What we Christians have received as the blessing of Abraham is the Spirit of Him who raised Jesus from among the dead. It is our birthright as the church of the firstborn to enter into the full realization of the God of resurrection as abundant grace. Such an experience will enrich our Christian life and service.

Section Outline

Part 5: Reigning in Life Today

Section Introduction

22. The reigning life of Christ
- o   Reigning in the crucified life of Christ
- o   Responding in faith, hope and love
- o   Proof of the reigning life of Christ

23. An overview of the kingdom in Scripture
- o   The kingdom is God's desire and intention in creation
- o   The Old Testament is about a kingdom gained and lost
- o   The New Testament is about the reality of the kingdom
- o   The kingdom of God in the New Testament in two aspects
- o   The life process of the kingdom
- o   The dominion and authority of the kingdom
- o   The consummation of the kingdom

24. Grace and the God of Abraham, Isaac and Jacob
- o   Grace and the God of resurrection
- o   Grace and God's operation for the kingdom

25. Reigning in life in service for the kingdom
- o   The pattern of Jesus and the apostles
- o   The pattern of the apostle Paul

26. Judah and Tamar: Key application principles
- o   The kingdom as our inheritance and exercise
- o   According to principles in Genesis 38
- o   Richly and bountifully supplied for the kingdom

Conclusion

Reigning in Life Today

Section Introduction

Now we come to the experience of kingship in the story of Judah and Tamar as our birthright. It cannot be overemphasized that kingship in the second Testament is a divine concept that is qualitatively very different from the familiar notion of leadership in the world. As Jesus Himself has said, "You know that the rulers of the Gentiles lord it over them, and their great ones exercise authority over them. It shall not be so among you. But whoever would be great among you must be your servant, and whoever would be first among you must be your slave" (Matt. 20:25–27). Kingship in the second Testament is the living out of the life of the Son of Man "… who came not to be served but to serve, and to give his life as a ransom for many" (v. 28).

From the commencement of the second Testament age, Jesus stressed that His kingdom is not a kingdom that is constituted with the natural life of man. After revealing to Peter that He would give him the keys of the kingdom of heaven with the authority to bind and loose (Matt. 16:19); Jesus told His disciples, "If anyone would come after me, let him deny himself and take up his cross and follow me" (v. 24). The denial of the self (the natural life of man) is the key to living out the kingdom life. Given this counter intuitive connotation of divine kingship, who is sufficient for these things? As we will see, the life of the kingdom that is implied in Jesus' teaching has much to do with the God of Abraham, Isaac, and Jacob. This life is none other than the manifestation of resurrection in Jesus, the incarnated Son of God. In other words, the kingdom is constituted of the resurrection life of Christ, and this life comes forth through the denial of our natural life in servitude to others for the sake of the kingdom.

22. The reigning life of Christ

The evidence for such a life is with the God who raised Jesus from among the dead. The very God of resurrection who stands behind the hypothesis of Scripture—of the order, arrangement, and connection in the Triune God's move across both Testaments—is the basis for a Christian experience of the kingly life as lived out and defined by the Son. The Christian Scripture derives its authority and character from the God who in the person of the pre-incarnated Son has served mankind in the reconciliation since the onset of the fall of man. The pattern of this life is seen in God's move through the pre-incarnated Son in the first Testament; and it was lived out among men in the person of the incarnated Son in the four Gospels.

Jesus, the incarnated Son, the One who subsisted in the form of God, but did not regard equality with God a thing to be grasped—lived and served according to the shape of a cruciform life (Phil. 2:5–11). The paradigm of His life in reaching mankind is characterized by a pattern of "descending" and "ascending." First descend: having emptied Himself, Jesus took the form of a slave, became in the likeness of men, humbled Himself and became obedient even unto the death of the cross. Then and only then does He ascend: wherefore, God raised Him up and highly exalted Him above every name that is named. Herein is the "cookie cutter" of the life of the kingdom: that the One who descended and was raised has become the firstfruits of those who have fallen asleep (1 Cor. 15:20). This implies that those who belong to Jesus would also follow suit in the same pattern of death (Rom. 6:3–4), resurrection (1 Cor. 15:23) and exaltation (Eph. 1:20; 2:6). This is the cruciform mold of the life of the kingdom in the age of grace.

Reigning in the crucified life of Christ It follows that our exaltation is not before we have worked out our salvation (Phil. 2:12b) by living a life that is conformed to the mold of the crucified life of Christ—that we may know the power of His resurrection (3:10). Then according to the apostle Paul, the end will eventually come, when Jesus "... delivers the kingdom to God the Father after destroying every rule and every authority and power" (1 Cor. 15:24). Jesus' delivery of the kingdom to the Father is predicated upon our present subjection to the ruling life of Christ (Eph. 1:22–23, 4:15–16, Col. 1:18, 2:19). And so even today Jesus must "... reign *until* he has put all his enemies under his feet (*emphasis added in italics*)" (1 Cor. 15:25). The significance of the little word "until" is that for Jesus to reign, all things must presently be subjected to Him who is the head (v. 28) of the body (Eph. 1:19–23).

Our God is a God with a purpose, and His purpose is His divine intent according to His Triune being. God's triune intention is to subject all things to Christ that God may be all in all (vv. 10–11). The consummation of the heading up of all things in Christ is the eternal kingdom spoken of in Daniel chapter 2. It begins with a stone cut without human hand that is destined to strike down the kingdoms of this world—a stone that will become a great mountain that fills the whole earth (Dan. 2:34–35, 44–45; Rev. 11:15). Jesus is that stone cut without human hand (Matt. 16:15–18, 21:42; Mark 12:10; Luke 20:17; Acts 4:11; 1 Cor. 3:10–11; Eph. 2:20; 1 Pet. 2:6–7), in that He was slain by God from the foundation of the earth (Rev. 13:8). Upon this stone Christ will build His church (the new community of faith, Matt. 16:18); and the church is His body, the fullness of Him who fills all in all. As such God's divine being and His triadic move and eternal operation to put all things in subjection to Christ in resurrection are defining characteristics of Christian Scripture and must govern the structure of our experience in reigning in Christ's life.

Responding in faith, hope and love Consequently, in keeping with the character of God and His operation, the principle of *regula fidei* must also *rule* our experience of Him who stands behind the order and pattern of Scripture. What makes our existential realization of God genuinely Christian is dictated by the nature of God and His purpose; the identity of the man He created; and

His move and operation in us for His intention. In initiating the recovery of Judah through Tamar, the God of Abraham, Isaac and Jacob acted according to the pattern of His Son, the pre-incarnated Christ of God. From our perspective, we need to see and respond (in faith and love) to all that God is in Christ (our hope) in the unveiling of Scripture as revelation across both Testaments. We affirm through our life, living and service that authentic Christian experience is our response in faith and love to who God is in His intrinsic being and work; and who God is, is Christ in us—our hope of glory (1 Cor. 13:8, Col. 1:27).

Thus our experience of the God of Abraham, Isaac, and Jacob is our response in faith, hope, and love to the God of the fathers— who acted in their calling, blessing and transformation. This is to have the mind of Christ in working out our salvation by cooperating with the God of resurrection within us as the Spirit, that we may participate in God's continuing recovery of kingship among men (Phil. 2:5, 12–14). And our affirmative response in faith elicits God's dynamic operation within us in resurrection as grace for His intended purpose that mankind may rule and reign on His behalf, even today—until all things are brought under subjection to Christ, that God may be all in all.

Proof of the reigning life of Christ In all those who belong to Christ, there is a kingdom life that presides within them. What reigns over believers is not mere outward legality but the life of the One who is the end of the law to all those who believe (Rom. 10:4). What is it that authenticates the truthfulness of a Christian's experience of the reigning life of God in Christ within them today? The proof of the veracity of God and the truthfulness of a Christian's experience of the reigning life of Christ is not in the ivory tower of intellectual arguments nor endless academic propositions. Neither is it to be found in mere noetic apprehension of some knowledge about God, no matter how esoteric and dogmatic that body of knowledge may be. Mundane as it sounds, what counts before God at the end of the day is the willing and doing of His will, in and according to His revelation and move across both Testaments. Anyone who wills to do His will, *will know* the truth about the Son's teaching, whether it is of God or whether He speaks from Himself (John 7:17). *The doing of the will of God in grace is the proof that we live in the reality of the kingdom today.*

We should never forget that even after all the academic methods of exegesis has been exhausted—*only* the very God of Abraham, Isaac and Jacob who authenticates His actions in the order and arrangement of Scripture as canon can testify concerning the truthfulness of our experience of Him through the witnessing act of the Spirit within us (John 16:13–15; Rom. 8:14–16). In resurrection, God in Christ resides and moves within us as the Spirit; and we cooperate with His anointing by working out our salvation in fear and trembling, for it is God who operates in us both the willing and working for His good pleasure (Phil. 2:12–13). Therefore, the apostle Paul charged us to do all things according to God's operation within us without murmurings and reasonings (v. 14). Anything apart from this divine-human interchange between God and the humankind He created and redeemed (after having fallen away) is more imagination than genuine experience of the God of resurrection. In sum, the kingdom life in resurrection is a life of obedience to the leading of the indwelling Spirit that we received as the promise given to Abraham (Gal. 3:14; Rom. 14:17; Eph. 4:30) at the dawn of God's calling out to him and his progeny.

This is so, for in resurrection, the Spirit as the promise of Abraham has come into our being. As such Romans 8 testifies that the indwelling Spirit of God, Christ, the Spirit of Christ, and the Spirit of Him who raised Jesus from the dead, witnesses with our spirit that we are the children of God (Rom. 8:9–11, 16). To a Christian—the divine designations of God, Christ, the Spirit of Christ, the Spirit of Him who raised Jesus from the dead—are not the designations of multiple identities. In the mystery of the divine Trinity they are One God, manifested as the Spirit who indwells us today. And as many as are led by the Spirit of God, these are the sons of God (v. 14). Thus the apostle Paul locates the genuineness of Christian experience in our inheritance of God's promise to Abraham, in the Spirit we have received as our Christian heritage and birthright through Christ's death and resurrection. The Spirit who indwells believers is the Spirit of sonship; and so having this Spirit we become firstly children of God, then heirs of God and coheirs with Christ (vv. 9–11, 16–17). This in essence is our inheritance of the reigning life of Christ for the kingdom, that Abraham's descendants (both circumcised and uncircumcised) may inherit the earth (4:12–25).

23. An overview of the kingdom in Scripture

There is little doubt that the kingdom of God is an overarching theme in Scripture, and that it is crucial for our understanding of the significance of kingship as birthright in the story of Judah and Tamar. The concept of the kingdom begins with God's creation and intention in Genesis 1. There God created mankind in His own image and likeness and gave them His authority to rule over all created things. In God's creation two items are very important for the motif of kingdom in the divine record—one is the divine image and the other is the divine dominion and authority (Gen. 1:26–27). Mankind was created in the image of God in order to express God, and humankind has received God's authority to represent Him. God's desire is for created mankind to subdue the earth by expressing and representing who God is in His image and authority.

The kingdom is God's desire and intention in creation
In order to have the full image of God to express God and to realize the full authority of God to represent Him, we must have God as life in us. Therefore, in the first two chapters of Genesis, there is not only image and authority (Gen. 1:27–28), but also life, signified by the tree of life (2:9). The kingdom of God is a matter of the life of God as signified by the tree of life. And in as much as authority is a function of life—even so, divine authority issues from the dynamism of the life of God. Life and authority are matters relating to the kingdom of God. Unless we have God's life in Christ as the Spirit we cannot even see, much less enter the kingdom of God (John 3:3–7). Believers are those who have been born of this life. Having been born anew (v. 3) we must also mature in this life so that we can have the full authority to represent Him.

What in essence then is the kingdom of God?

It simply means the rule or government of God over His people. For a kingdom to exist there must be life of a certain kind as well as an authority that goes with that life. For God's kingdom to exist there must be a group of people with God's life under His full authority. We receive this life when we believe in Jesus, for John 1:12 reads, "But to all who did receive him, who believed in his name, he gave the right [authority] to become children of God." Being designated a child of God is a matter of birthright and authority that issues forth from having the life of God. This is so for verse 13 further elaborates on the intrinsic nature of the children of God, "**...** who *were born*, not of blood nor of the will of the flesh nor of the will of man, *but of God* [*emphasis in italics*]." We are those who have been born of God, and therefore have been committed with the life and authority of God as citizens of the kingdom of God. The citizens of a country have been vested with the life and authority of a human world. Likewise, the citizens of God's kingdom are those who have been committed with the life and authority of God. This is God's desire for us from the foundation of the world (Eph. 1:4–5). As such it is God's intention in creation in Genesis 1 and 2, even before the fall of man.

The Old Testament is about a kingdom gained and lost Thus the kingdom of God is a hidden realm constituted of the life of God. In the words of Jesus, it is like the treasure "... hidden in a field, which a man found and covered up. Then in his joy he goes and sells all that he has and buys that field" (Matt. 13:44). The hidden treasure of the life of God was there from the beginning. After being created, Adam and Eve was placed in the midst of the garden in which was the tree of life (Genesis 2:8–9), and they were charged to eat rightly (v. 16), but not of the tree of knowledge of good and evil (v. 17). The tree of life hidden in plain sight (being in the center of the garden) is God as the inner source of life for man. It is God embodied in Christ as life for the mankind He created in His image and likeness. It will in the fullness of time be revealed as the true vine in John 15:1. Jesus told His disciples, "I am the true vine, and my Father is the vinedresser [husbandman]. Every branch in me that does not bear fruit, he takes away; and every *branch* that does bear fruit, he prunes, that it may bear more fruit" (John 15:1–2).

God in Christ is the tree of life and we are the many branches in Him as the true vine tree. God in Christ is the source and we are the issue. But before God could come into Adam and Eve as life and carry out His purpose, the subtle serpent caused mankind to fall by deceiving them to eat of the fruit of the tree of knowledge of good and evil instead of the tree of life (Gen. 3:1–6). Due to the Fall, the race of Adam failed God, so He chose Noah, then Abraham. According to Genesis 12:13, God chose Abraham with the definite intention of having a kingdom. God promised to make Abraham a great nation. This means God would make of him a kingdom, a nation of people with God as the source of life. In Old Testament parlance, that symbiotic relationship between God and His people was captured using the image of another tree. Hence the apostle Paul referred to the nation of Israel as the cultivated olive tree (Rom. 9:24). The One who cultivated Israel as a nation over the millennia is the God of their fathers—the God of Abraham, Isaac and Jacob. In the second Testament, this imagery would be replaced by that of God the Father as the husbandman, God the Son as the true vine, and the new community of faith as the branches in the vine (John 15:1, 5).

God chose Abraham and his descendants to be a nation—a kingdom with Himself as the source. This is how the people of Israel came into being. After the Lord brought the people of Israel out of Egypt, He said to them that they shall be to Him a kingdom of priests, and a holy nation (Exo. 19:6). The entire first Testament is a depiction of God's continuing work to gain this kingdom: the conquest of the good land under Joshua and Caleb; the period of anarchy in Judges; climaxing with the kingship of David; to the divided kingdom of Israel after Solomon; the Babylonian exile of the children of Israel; and their return from exile under Zerubbabel, Ezra and Nehemiah. Whenever the people of God held on to Him as the source of life, the kingdom was there. And when they departed from God, the kingdom was lost. As a record of the cultivated olive tree, the first Testament is the story of the continuing struggle between God and His people told as the saga of a kingdom gained, lost, regained and lost again.

The New Testament is about the reality of the kingdom So when the second Testament opens we see a kingdom lost again, for God's people were at that time under Roman rule. Amidst their loss, when John the Baptist came preaching, he first announced, "Repent, for the kingdom of heaven is at hand" (Matt. 3:2). When the Lord Jesus went out to preach, He said exactly the same thing, "Repent, for the kingdom of heaven is at hand" (4:17). When the twelve disciples were sent out in Luke 9 and the seventy disciples in Luke 10, Jesus told them to preach concerning the kingdom. From Matthew to Revelation, the subject of the kingdom comes up again and again. Its centrality in the divine thought is unmistakable, for the words "kingdom" "kingdom of God" or "kingdom of heaven" in its various forms occur more than three hundred times in the second Testament.

In Revelation, at the consummation of Scripture, we are told that the kingdom of the world has become the kingdom of our Lord and of His Christ, and He shall reign forever and ever. The first Adam may have failed, but the Lord Jesus as the last Adam (1 Cor. 15:45) will gain a kingdom for God and will rule as king over God's people eternally. The counsel and determination of our God is such that the kingdom of this world *will* become the kingdom of our Lord and of His Christ, and we who first believed *will* reign with Him forever (Rev. 11:15, 20:6, 22:5). Thus at the very end of Scripture we can see that God will eventually have a kingdom in which He can exercise His authority to the fullest extent in accomplishing His eternal purpose—by gaining a group of people committed with His life and authority. This is the new community of faith who takes God as the source of all that they are and do; even as the branches takes the true vine tree as the source of its very life, being and existence. This is the reality of the kingdom in the second Testament.

The kingdom of God in the New Testament in two aspects

There is a sense in which the entire universe and all that it contains—both animate and inanimate—is a part of the kingdom of God.

God's purpose however, is not just with His creation in general. More specifically, His kingdom is with the highest order of creation, the human race He endowed with His image and likeness. So the kingdom of God is not just with the world in a general way, but it was manifested as the outward realm of God's ruling activity with Israel in the first Testament. In the second Testament, the kingdom is the inward realm of God's intimate ruling and reigning through God's life from within believers as the Spirit. God's ruling and reigning from within His people has an issue—the manifestation of His divine authority, power and dominion over everything else extrinsically.

This implies *firstly* that the kingdom in the second Testament is a matter of life—God's life in Christ as the Spirit within the believers. And *secondly*, as God's people subject themselves to the ruling life of Christ; God's kingdom is manifested as His authority and power over His people specifically, and by extension over all else in totality. Both items—life and authority—are dual aspects of the kingdom in the second Testament. Life and authority are intimately connected to God's resurrection life in Christ that believers have received as the Spirit (Gal. 3:14). The Spirit who indwells us is the Spirit of life (Rom. 8:2); and God's divine authority stands behind those who are subjected to the ruling of the Spirit, for as many as are led by the Spirit, these are the sons of God (v. 14), and fellow heirs of Christ (v. 17). Thus the promise of the Spirit given to Abraham, Isaac and Jacob points retrospectively back to God's creation of man in His image and likeness—that mankind was created with the expressed purpose of receiving God as life that they may express God's image and represent His authority as revealed in Genesis 1–2.

For this reason, in disputing with the Corinthian believers who claimed that there is no resurrection of the dead; the apostle Paul presented his demonstration of God's resurrection life in the context of Christ having been raised as the precursor to all who will similarly be resurrected. Having been raised as the firstfruits, God in Christ is now ruling in resurrection in all those who are being saved—until He has put all His enemies under His feet by abolishing all rule, and all authority and power—by which time Christ will hand over the kingdom to His God and Father (1 Cor. 15:20-26). At its consummation, even death, mankind's last enemy would have been defeated (v. 26). In the apostle's mind, the very process of God's complete salvation in life (see the following section on the "The life process of the kingdom") that believers are undergoing is proof of the dynamism of the resurrection life of Christ that is even now operating in Abraham's heirs for the consummation of the kingdom. And all these things are made possible because in resurrection, the last Adam (Christ) became a life-giving Spirit (15:45b).

The life process of the kingdom From the perspective of a believer's inner life, the process of the kingdom in the second Testament begins with the coming of Jesus. This is so, for Christ is our life (Col. 3:4), and as such He is the seed of the kingdom. In Mark 4:26–29, the Lord Jesus likened the kingdom to a man who sows seed into the earth. The seed grows, the blade appears, the ear appears, and finally it is harvested. In this parable, the kingdom is presented as a seed that is sown into the earth, and that grows until it reaches maturity; at which time it will be harvested (Rev. 14:15). Cleary then, the Lord Jesus is the seed of the aforementioned kingdom. He is the seed of life of the kingdom—the grain of wheat that was sown into the earth, dies and in turn bears much fruit (John 12:24). We are the many grains or fruit brought forth in His death and resurrection through our regeneration (John 3:3, 5–8) when we believe (1:12–13).

Our new birth is indeed a divine mystery!

Jesus told a puzzled Nicodemus in John 3:7–8, "Do not marvel that I said to you, 'You must be born again.' The wind blows where it wishes, and you hear its sound, but you do not know where it comes from or where it goes. So it is with everyone who is born of the Spirit." Being born of the Spirit is not something that can be substantiated with the physical senses. It is a matter of believers having received the resurrection life of God in Christ as the Spirit when they were regenerated. In Jesus' own words, "... that which is born of the Spirit is spirit" (v. 6). Put another way, Jesus is saying that, that which is born of the Spirit of God is the spirit of man. A divine transaction transpires in the depths of our human spirit at the moment we believe that is invisible to human physical senses.

So the second Testament tells us that the kingdom of God does not come with observation (Luke 17:20–21). There is nothing natural about this kingdom that the worldly eyes can see. We enter into this kingdom through the first step of God's salvation in life—regeneration, by believing in Christ. Regeneration is the Lord Jesus as the Spirit coming into our human spirit as the seed of life to give us all things pertaining to life and godliness (2 Peter 1:4). The wonder of wonders is that all things pertaining to the kingdom of God has been given to us. When we cooperate with Him as the indwelling Spirit, the seed of the kingdom that has been sown into us grows and develops. It is in this way that we are provided with a rich entrance into the kingdom—not just an entrance but a rich entrance.

To reiterate, the kingdom of God thus begins with Jesus as the seed of life. After having received Him, the pathway of the kingdom for believers is the process of God's complete salvation in life (Rom. 5:10). In the second Testament, salvation in life is a six-step life process that starts with our regeneration as the initiation, and our growth in life in the Spirit as the life pathway for the kingdom:

1. Regeneration & renewing (Titus 3:5; John 1:13; 3:3, 16, 36a; Rom. 12:2b, Titus 3:5c; 2 Cor. 5:17; Gal 6:15);

2. Sanctification & transformation (Rom. 6:19, 22; 15:16; 2 Pet. 1:4; Rom; 12:2a; 2 Cor. 3:18);

3. Conformation & glorification (Rom. 8:29; 1 John 3:2; Rom. 8:30, 23; Eph. 4:30; Phil. 3:21; Col. 3:4b; 1 Peter 5:10a; 2 Tim. 2:10; Heb. 2:10)

The life processes of regeneration, renewing, sanctification, conformation and glorification spells out what all Christians must pass through to become fully conformed to the firstborn Son of God (Rom. 8:28). Thus the apostle Paul wrote in Romans 5:10 that much more, having been reconciled—we shall be *saved by (or in) His life*. On the one hand we are already saved in that our eternal destiny before God is positionally secure, for our sins have been judicially forgiven when we believed in Jesus' death on the cross (3:24, 10:9–10). But Christ not only died for our sins. He also rose from the dead that we may have His life, and be justified by this life (4:25). 1 Corinthians 15:45b clearly states that the last Adam [Christ] became a live-giving Spirit in resurrection. It is as the Spirit that the resurrected Christ now indwells us as life (Rom. 8:9–10). This is the life-giving Spirit that believers have received as the promise of Abraham through faith (Gal. 3:14).

And so the children of God are those who have received the Spirit of life, and are now undergoing the process of God's salvation in life. We are passing through the life processes of God's salvation that we may be saved to the uttermost in Christ's life. And at every stage of God's salvation in life, the indwelling Spirit is the key for our experience. The goal of God's salvation in life is for every part of our being to be permeated with the life of the Spirit: our mind, spirit, and body all come to life (Rom. 8:6, 10–11 NASB) that God may be all in all. Sin and death reigns in fallen mankind; but in the economy of God's salvation, *much more* we who receive the abundance of grace and of the gift of righteousness *will reign in life* through the One, Jesus Christ—so that, as sin reigned in death, even so grace might reign through righteousness to eternal life through Jesus Christ our Lord (Rom. 5:17, 21). The issue of God's full salvation in life is our reigning in Christ's life, and our reigning in life brings us into the reality of the kingdom life in the church—the life of the body of Christ as the one new man.

There is thus a corporate manifestation to our experience of salvation in life that is related to God's kingdom. The apostle Paul developed this fully using the imagery of the body of Christ and the one new man. As we grow in Christ we grow up into Him as the Head in all things; and out from Him the whole body, being fitted and held together by that which every joint supply, according to the proper working of each individual part, causes the growth of the body for the building up of itself in love (Eph. 4:15–16). We see here the Pauline representation of the Johannine branches and the true vine (John 15:1). The Father cultivates the true vine tree and the branches grow by abiding in the vine. The two together, the true vine and the branches; Christ the Head and the believers as His body, constitute the one new man (Eph. 2:15, 4:24; Col. 3:10), where He as the Head is the "KING" and we, the body—is the "DOM", the domain for God to exercise His ruling. And this one new man is the highest expression of the KING-DOM of God as the goal of the economy of God's salvation in Christian Scripture.

The dominion and authority of the kingdom

The existence of the one new man requires not only life within but also authority without. Having been born of the Spirit, the new man has life within. However, there is still the need for the new man—where Christ is the Head and we the believers are the one body—to be inaugurated into the kingship that the new man may share in Christ's authority and power (Matt. 28:18–20; Acts 1:4, 5, 8). This is reminiscent of the anointing of Aaron as High Priest in the first Testament. In the words of Psalms 133:2–3, "It is like the precious oil on the head, running down on the beard, on the beard of Aaron, running down on the collar of his robes. It is like the dew of Hermon, which falls on the mountains of Zion! For there the Lord has commanded the blessing, life forever."

At the beginning of Jesus' ministry in the four gospels, we see the Spirit coming upon Jesus (Matt. 3:17; Mark 3:10; Luke 3:22; 4:18; John 1:32). That was the anointing of Christ as the Head of the body. Then in Acts we witness the promise of the Spirit coming upon the Jewish and Gentile parts of the body (Acts 1:8; 2:4; 10:44). That was the anointing flowing down from the Head to the body that the body may share in Christ's dominion, authority and power. With the baptism of the Holy Spirit in Acts, the promise given to the fathers concerning the seed of the woman has been fully realized (Gen. 3:15). Today this wonderful person has come. As the rightful king, He is the reality of kingship and the constituting element of the kingdom of God. In Luke 11, when some accused Jesus that He cast out demons by Beelzebul, the prince of demons, Jesus replied, "But if it is by the finger of God that I cast out demons, then the kingdom of God has come upon you" (Luke 11:18). The kingdom is centered upon Him as the reality and the content.

With this brief survey of the kingdom of God in Scripture, we can better appreciate the significance of the first Testament as pointing forward to the coming of Jesus as heir to the kingdom of David. Thus, the Gospel of Matthew, the first book of the second Testament opens with Jesus' name, "The book of the genealogy of Jesus Christ, the son of David, the son of Abraham" (Matt. 1:1), clearly establishing Him as the rightful heir to the throne of David. As we have seen, Genesis 38 was written with this divine goal in view. The birthright and kingship in the story of Judah and Tamar is related to Jesus as the rightful heir to David's throne. The kingdom of David finds its continuation with Jesus in the second

Testament. For this very reason, Matthew at its very beginning presents the genealogy of Jesus Christ (Matt. 1:1–16) as the summary of the first Testament in forty-two generations (v. 17), leading to "Now the birth of Jesus Christ took place in this way ..." (v. 18).

The consummation of the kingdom The person of Jesus Christ and all that He does is the kingdom. The believers' inheritance of kingship in the kingdom is related to their experience of reigning with Christ in the church today as the kingdom of God. And their participation in the reigning life of Christ as the indwelling Spirit has a consummation. Revelation is a book on the manifestation of the kingdom of God in all its glory and power. At the end of the age when the seventh angel blew his trumpet, there will be a loud voice in heaven saying, "The kingdom of the world has become the kingdom of our Lord and of his Christ, and he shall reign forever and ever" (Rev. 11:15). The final book of Christian Scripture presents Jesus as the King of kings (17:4; 19:6). It is the destiny of Christians to rule and reign with Christ their king. The words delivered to the messenger of the church in Thyatira (as with the other six churches in Revelation 2–3) was a call for believers to overcome the degraded situation of the church: "The one who conquers [overcomes] and who keeps my works until the end, to him I will give authority over the nations, and he will rule them with a rod of iron, as when earthen pots are broken in pieces, even as I myself have received authority from my Father (2:26–27)".

This call for believers to overcome is directed at all Christians for the Lord has "... made them a kingdom and priests to our God, and they shall reign on the earth" (5:10). We may not have much realization concerning the reality of reigning with Christ today, but the divine fact is that our universe is on a rendezvous with the kingdom of God and of His Christ. A day will come when "... the night will be no more. They will need no light of lamp or sun, for the Lord God will be their light, and they will reign forever and ever." (22:5). As Christians, we believe these verses, yet we are likely to put off its realization to a distant tomorrow that is only vaguely relevant in this life.

24. Grace and the God of Abraham, Isaac and Jacob

John 11 tells of a certain Lazarus in Bethany who was taken ill. His sister Martha put out words to Jesus in the hope that his brother would be healed. But when Jesus delayed, Lazarus died. When a disappointed Martha heard Jesus say, "Your brother will rise again" (v. 23), she immediately responded with a doctrinal understanding that postponed Jesus' statement to a distant tomorrow, for she said, "I know that he will rise again in the resurrection on the last day" (v. 24). Jesus corrected her with the words, "I *am* the resurrection and the life (*emphasis added in italics*)" (v. 25). What Jesus said was not some doctrinal statement about Himself as resurrection and life for tomorrow. Jesus is the resurrection and the life, even now, for our experience. But like Martha before us, we are as likely to postpone our experience of reigning in Christ's resurrection life to a distant future according to our doctrinal understanding of kingship.

The hidden God in the story of Judah and Tamar is the God of Abraham, Isaac, and Jacob. He is the One who called Abraham out from the land of idolaters to a better country, a heavenly city[1] (Heb. 11:10, 15–16; Rev. 21:14, 19). God promised that Abraham would become a father of many nations—in line with God's original intention that the man He created would rule and reign on His behalf. Abraham's response to God is his experience of the God of resurrection who calls and promises. In Abraham's spiritual experiences with respect the conception and sacrifice of his son Isaac—God is the God who gives life to the dead and calls the things not being as being (Gen. 17:5; 18:11, 14; Rom. 4:17; Heb. 11:11–12, 18). The highest point of Abraham's spiritual journey with God is seen in Genesis 22; in his obedience to God's command to sacrifice Isaac, his only son. In that one command, God brings to remembrance for the sake of posterity that from nothing He has called Isaac into being; and now in the patriarch's sacrifice of his only son (begotten with Sarah), Abraham would experience in figure the power of the God of resurrection—the very God who gives life to the dead.

Grace and the God of resurrection   Resurrection is the quintessential nature of the God of Abraham, Isaac, and Jacob; and by implication it is also the basis for the patriarchs' experience of Him. For this reason Jesus invoked the title of the God of Abraham,

---

1. Hebrews reveals that the better country Abraham sought was a heavenly one, a city that had the foundations, whose Architect and Builder was God. Today this heavenly city is the church of the firstborn, the city of the living God with Christ as foundation (Matt. 16:18; 1 Cor. 3:9–12; Heb. 12:22–23), where we have been seated in the heavenlies with Christ (Eph. 1:3, 20–22). Its final consummation will be the New Jerusalem, the eternal city of God and His redeemed with twelve foundations (Rev. 21:14, 19).

Isaac and Jacob to prove to the Sadducees that there is such a thing as the resurrection of the dead. This is because in Jesus' divine logic, God is not the God of the dead but of the living (Matt. 22:31–32). It follows then that in the eyes of the God of resurrection, the patriarchs are not dead but living. Thus Abraham's offering up of Isaac in Genesis 22 was Abraham's experience of the God of resurrection. Abraham the father, considered that God was able even to raise Isaac from the 'dead' (Heb. 11:19); and Isaac, the son was obedient even unto 'death' (Gen. 22:4–13). And so Abraham received Isaac back in resurrection, and through his experience of the God of resurrection; Isaac as the one grain became Jacob, and from Jacob would come the twelve tribes of Israel (the house of Jacob). The apostle Paul referred to this as Abraham's experience of the God "who gives life to the dead and calls into existence the things that do not exist" (Rom. 4:17).

In time Isaac as the one grain that Abraham received back in resurrection would become as numerous as the stars of heaven and the sand on the seashore (Gen. 22:17, Rom. 9:27, Heb. 11:12). All these issued from Abraham's response in faith to the God of resurrection. In the second Testament, the Lord would allude to this concerning His own death and resurrection: "Truly, truly, I say to you, unless a grain of wheat falls into the earth and dies, it abides alone, but if it dies, it bears much fruit." What Abraham experienced in figure in Genesis, finally came to fruition in Christ as the single grain of wheat that dies and brought forth many grains in resurrection.

Thus the second Testament relates the God of the patriarchs explicitly to the God of resurrection. All three references to the God of Abraham, Isaac, and Jacob in the Synoptics (Matthew, Mark and Luke) were quoted by the Lord in the context of God's resurrection power (Matt. 22:32, Mark 12:26, Luke 20:37). This proved that Abraham experienced the God of resurrection in figure when he offered up his only begotten *son,* whom he received through promise—the one of whom it was said, "Through Isaac shall your offspring be named" (Heb. 11:17–19). The second Testament reveals that our experience of the God of Abraham, Isaac, and Jacob is the experience of the God of resurrection in reality, in the Son—that is, in Christ Jesus who died and rose again. In resurrection Christ justifies, regenerates, indwells, sanctifies, and glorifies the believers. And so the apostle Paul says that to know Him is to know the power of His resurrection (Phil. 3:10), being conformed to His death.

Grace and God's operation for the kingdom It is in terms of the God of resurrection that grace in the second Testament should be understood. Grace is much more than just "unmerited favor" as we commonly understands it. While unmerited favor does carry some of the significance of grace, that description lacks richness in conveying the full import of biblical grace. In the first Testament, the God of Abraham, Isaac, and Jacob operated outside the patriarchs; but today in the second Testament, He operates within us, now that we have received the blessing of Abraham—that is the promise of the Spirit by faith.

The promise of Abraham as the Spirit is our inheritance, our birthright. Akin to the cooperation Judah and Tamar rendered in Genesis 38 to gain the birthright; we need to respond to the indwelling Spirit with our obedience—so we may go on to experience the saving operation of the God of Abraham, Isaac, and Jacob within us, that God may complete the good work He began (Phil. 1:6). This is the application of the varied grace of the God of Abraham, Isaac, and Jacob to our Christian life for the goal of conforming us to the firstborn Son of God, that we may participate in the work of reconciliation in the kingdom (even as Judah must have experienced when he *prevailed*, i.e., *gabar*, over his brothers to serve them). So the connotation of grace goes much deeper than just unmerited favor. It is that for sure but then also much more.

In the deepest sense, grace is none other than the present saving operation of the God of Abraham, Isaac, and Jacob within us as the indwelling Spirit in resurrection. What we Christians inherited as the blessing of Abraham is the Spirit of Him who raised Christ Jesus from the dead (Gal. 3:14; Rom. 8:11). In this respect, the apostle Paul charged the Philippians to render their cooperation to God by working out their salvation with fear and trembling, for it was God Himself who operated[2] in them—both the willing

---

2. Greek *energeia* can be translated as work or energize or operate. This term was used by the apostle Paul extensively to indicate the active and powerful operation of God the Spirit within New Testament believers (Eph. 1:19–20; Gal 2:8; 1 Cor. 12:4–6, 11; 2 Cor. 1:6; 4:12; Eph. 3:20; Phil. 2:13; Col. 1:29; Eph. 3:7–11; 4:15–16, among others). Some scholars are of the opinion that *operation* is too impersonal for use in translating the Greek *energeia*. There is no doubt that the Spirit of God is not an impersonal power but the third person of the Godhead. But perhaps we should also remember that Paul viewed the experience of the indwelling Spirit in Romans 8 as the outworking of the law of the Spirit of life, as opposed to the law of sin and death. The emphasis, I think,

and the working for His good pleasure (Phil. 2:12–13). This does not mean that having been saved by faith in Jesus, the apostle is now charging them to be saved by works. What it does mean is that they have received the God of Abraham, Isaac, and Jacob into them as the indwelling Spirit. And the indwelling Spirit within them is not passive; much rather, He is powerful and operative to work out their salvation (which requires their obedience and cooperation, v. 12) so they may be conformed to the self-emptying and self-humbling life pattern of the Son (vv. 5–8).

As elaborated on previously, this is conformation to the saving pattern of Him who existed in the form of God but did not regard equality with God a thing to be grasped. But rather, taking the form of a slave, becoming in the likeness of men, and being found in fashion as a man, He became obedient even unto death, and that the death of a cross. As a result God highly exalted Him and bestowed on Him the name that is above every name "so that in the name of Jesus every knee should bow, in heaven and on earth and under the earth, and every tongue confess that Jesus Christ

---

is not on "personal" versus "impersonal" but rather on the spontaneous operation and function of a powerful law, the law of the Spirit of God within the believers. The sense in Romans 8 is that when the conditions are fulfilled, God will spontaneously operate within the believers, even as sin operates as a spontaneous law within fallen man, making him a captive to sin (Romans 7). The conditions for the law of the Spirit of life to function are spelled out as setting our minds on the Spirit, having our being according to the Spirit, walking by the Spirit, being witnessed to by the Spirit, and being led by the Spirit—conditions that are descriptive of an intimate and personal relationship with the indwelling Spirit within believers. And so, in keeping with the apostle Paul's accent on the spontaneous energizing capacity and functioning of God's operation as grace within the believers, I see no issue in using *operation* to translate *energeia* in most contexts. On the contrary, besides the semantic link to spontaneity, the word *operate* also conveys something very vital and dynamic about the Spirit's function within believers as opposed to just "work," which carries a connotation that is rather commonplace today.

is Lord, to the glory of God the Father" (vv. 9–11). This is the God-ordained pathway of kingship that Jesus took on His way to exaltation by God. If we would experience the full import of grace, our Christian life and service must of necessity conform to the self-emptying and self-humbling pattern of Jesus' life in service to God's kingdom.

Consequently, grace is not just unmerited favor.

It is the power of God in resurrection for our Christian living and service. The surpassing greatness of this power was what accounted for the apostle Paul's exuberance when he prayed for the Ephesians that God would grant them a spirit of wisdom and revelation in the knowledge of Him—that the eyes of their hearts would be enlightened, that they may know what are the riches of His *glorious inheritance* in the saints (Eph. 1:17–18). God's "glorious inheritance" in the saints is the life issue of their experience of the "immeasurable greatness of power" that is granted to all who believe (v. 18a). This power works in the believers according to the very operation of the might of God's strength, which He caused to operate in Christ when He raised Him "from the dead and seated him at his right hand in the heavenly places, far above all rule and authority and power and dominion, and above every name that is named, not only in this age but also in the one to come" (vv. 20–21).

And it is this dynamic power of resurrection that has subjected all things under Christ's feet and has given Him to be the Head over all things to the church, which is His body, the fullness of Him who fills all in all (vv. 18b–23). This is grace, as the operation of God's might upon the man Jesus that has accomplished so much in Him (and will accomplish even more in the church as the kingdom, John 14:10–12; Eph. 3:20). And the basis for our experience of the resurrection power that is now in us as the Spirit is the self-emptying and self-humbling pattern of Jesus' life that leads to God's exaltation of Him. The self-emptying and self-humbling mold of Jesus' life is for our learning (Eph. 4:20–21) that we may reign in His life for our service in the kingdom of God.

This is how the apostle Paul understood the pattern and mold of his laboring among the Gentiles and for the kingdom in fulfilling the ministry of reconciliation entrusted to him. In Galatians, the apostle said that He who operated in Peter for his apostolic ministry to the circumcised, operated also in Paul for his ministry to the Gentiles (Gal. 2:8). According to Paul, the apostles labored not in themselves but according to their experience of grace that operated in them in power.

25. Reigning in life in service for the kingdom

God's actions in us follow the characteristics of His life and nature. The pattern of His life and ways are imprinted in His acts in the first and second Testaments of Christian Scripture. The move of the pre-incarnated Christ in the story of Judah and Tamar bears the imprint of His footsteps in His incarnated acts in the second Testament. What then do we see in the second Testament that we would otherwise have missed in our reading of Genesis 38?

The pattern of Jesus and the apostles We see Jesus, the incarnated Son, seeking the lost sheep of the house of Israel. The imagery of Christ as the shepherd in the second Testament is visible everywhere in His ministry (before and after resurrection and even in ascension), in which He carries out God's own ministry of reconciliation. In contrast to the tyrant Herod, Christ is the ruler who will *shepherd* His people, Israel (Matt. 2:6). At the beginning of His ministry, He was concerned for the people who were distressed and dispirited like sheep without a shepherd (Matt. 9:36). In His ministry in incarnation, Christ shepherded the lost sheep of the house of Israel by seeking the one lost sheep (Luke 15:4–7). He was the door for the sheep to go in and out to find pasture (John 10:2–5). He gathered them together as one flock (John 10:16). He was the good shepherd who took care of God's flock by laying down His life for them (John 10:9–15, 17–18). Dying on the cross was Christ being struck down as the shepherd, followed by the scattering of the flock (Matt. 26:31).

In resurrection He charged Peter to feed His lambs and shepherd His sheep (John 21:15–17). The apostle Paul charged the elders in Ephesus to guard the flock, to shepherd the church of God, which God purchased with His own blood (Acts 20:28). The apostle Peter was so deeply impressed with who the Lord was as the shepherd that he brought it to remembrance when he admonished the elders in his first epistle, that they were to shepherd the flock of God, according to God (not according to themselves)—not by lording it over them but by becoming patterns of the flock. In this way, Peter adds, "When the Chief

Shepherd appears, you will receive the unfading crown of glory" (1 Peter 5:4).

These aspects of God in Christ as our shepherd are so significant that the Epistle to the Hebrews designate it as the purpose of the Lord's resurrection by the blood of the eternal covenant (Heb. 13:20). The concluding word to the Hebrews says, "Now may the God of peace who brought again from the dead our Lord Jesus, the great shepherd of the sheep, by the blood of the eternal covenant, equip you with everything good that you may do His will, working in us that which is pleasing in His sight, through Jesus Christ, to whom *be* the glory forever and ever. Amen" (vv. 20–21). The Book of Revelation reveals that even in ascension, Christ will be recognized as the shepherd, "For the Lamb in the midst of the throne will be their shepherd, and will guide them to springs of living water, and God will wipe every tear from their eyes" (Rev. 7:17).

This way of talking about God in Christ in the second Testament makes it inevitable that we read Genesis 38 as the pre-incarnated Son in His move to seek Judah through Tamar's actions—an ascription we might otherwise have missed. And we can take Judah and Tamar's response to God's move in their situation as a response that merits our attention. Although God is righteous and abhors sin and wickedness (as seen in the killing of Onan and Err), He sought and recovered Judah as a shepherd according to His love and promise to Abraham and His intention for man in creation.

The pattern of the apostle Paul Though the apostle Paul was least among the apostles (not even worthy to be called such), in that he persecuted the church of God, he testified that he labored more abundantly than all the rest, "though it was not I, but the grace of God that is with me" (1 Cor. 15:9–10). The grace that was given to him was not in vain because he cooperated fully with God's mighty operation within him obediently (Acts 26:12–20). He said to the saints in Colosse and Laodecia that the apostles struggled with this operation, which worked in them in power that they may proclaim Christ, warning everyone and teaching everyone with all wisdom that they may present everyone mature in Christ (Col. 1:28–29).

There are too many instances for us to mistake what the apostle Paul meant when he said, "not I but Christ," and "not I but the grace of God." He was witnessing to an inward operation (Gal. 2:8; 2 Cor. 4:12; Eph. 3:20; Phil. 2:13; Col. 1:29; Eph. 1:19–23 and so on) arising from the indwelling Spirit of God, Christ, the Spirit of Christ that operated within him to energize, empower, and enable him to fulfill his obligations in the kingdom. Consequently he could testify, "I can do all things in Him who strengthens [empowers] me" (Phil. 4:13). In case some would claim that such an experience in laboring according to God's operation as grace was directed only to the apostles, or maybe just the "professional" servants of God as we call them today, let us be reminded that all believers are to labor and walk according to the apostles as our example and pattern, and in turn we are to be a model to others (2 Thess. 3:9; 1 Tim. 4:12; Titus 2:7; 1 Pet. 5:3).

Such a labor according to God's operation is a labor in the kingdom and for the kingdom. It is what kingship means in service, for to serve in this way is to prevail as Judah did—to overcome, to contend, to rise up, to stand above all contrary situations and circumstances to serve others—and cooperate with grace according to the triune operation of God to energize us (2 Cor. 4:7–12). The treasure in us, as the earthen vessel (that is Christ in us as our hope of glory, Col. 1:27), is the source of the surpassing greatness of His power in our service.

The apostle Paul testified descriptively of his experience of grace as the power of resurrection in his prevailing over every circumstances in these words: "*We are* afflicted in every way, but not crushed; perplexed, but not driven to despair; persecuted, but not forsaken; struck down, but not destroyed" (2 Cor. 4:8–9). It is in this manner that the apostle carried out his ministry of reconciliation in and for the kingdom, by being conformed to the dying of Jesus in his body, that the life of Jesus also would be manifested in resurrection to those he ministered to in his service to God. It was in this pattern of death and resurrection that the apostles were being delivered over to death for Jesus's sake, so that the life of Jesus would be manifested in their mortal flesh. So Paul said, "Death is at work in us, but life in you" (v. 12).

26. Judah and Tamar: Key application principles

What are we to do in the face of such revelation of grace and the kingdom in the word of God? As the apostle Peter charged, God's divine power has granted us all things pertaining to life and godliness. These are precious and exceedingly great promises that we may become partakers of the divine nature (2 Pet. 1:3–4). This is our inheritance, our birthright, as the church of the firstborn, and it is a gift of grace. So what do we do? Having been so gifted, we should render to God our obedience and cooperation. Rather than being idle and unfruitful, we are to add all diligence to this foundation of grace—and supply bountifully in our faith, virtue; and in virtue, knowledge; and in knowledge, self-control; and in self-control, endurance; and in endurance, godliness; and in godliness, brotherly love; and in brother love, love (vv. 4–7).

The kingdom as our inheritance and exercise Our exercise in the kingdom is not based on our own effort and what we are in ourselves. It is based on "these things" (v. 8) that have been granted to us—that is, the aforementioned virtues that already exist in us (for we have been granted all things relating to life and godliness)—that we may be constituted neither idle nor unfruitful in the full knowledge of Him (v. 8). In relation to our exercise, "these things" exist in us, even as all the fullness of a flower is contained within its genes. In the same way, the fullness of the kingdom is contained in Jesus, who is within us as the hope of glory within. Therefore, as in Judah who repented and went back to the house of Jacob to exercise his kingship in prevailing over his brothers to serve them in reconciliation for the kingdom, we should go and do likewise.

The story of Judah and Tamar, in light of the second Testament in Jesus, highlights a need for right association with Christ based on the pattern of His death and resurrection as the pathway of kingship in the kingdom. The characteristics of this relationship are defined by who God is in Christ; His intention and ordination for man, as well as man's response to Him; and His move in them. Tamar's seeking of the birthright is her response to God's heart and move in her situation. Judah likewise responded, for he confessed and repented and went back to his brothers to serve them in the reconciliation.

The God of Abraham, Isaac, and Jacob, who was present in Judah and Tamar's situation, is within us today as the God of resurrection. As the Spirit of Him who raised Jesus from the dead, God is within us as our grace. Grace is none other than the living, active, and powerful operation of the God of Abraham, Isaac, and Jacob in us. In inheriting the blessing of Abraham, we have been brought into the move and operation of the God of the patriarchs for the constitution of the kingdom of God. The same God who acted for the kingship in Judah and Tamar in Genesis 38 is operative within us for the same purpose. The character of Christian Scripture is comprised of the triadic God of Abraham, Isaac, and Jacob who is now the God of resurrection who indwells us as the Spirit.

According to principles in Genesis 38 As such, we can discern certain principles in Genesis 38 that are applicable to our experience in light of the revelation of Christ in the second Testament that requires a response from us. In this regard, Goldingay says, "Reading the first Testament Christologically then can mean letting who Jesus is give us clues to a right reading of the way the first Testament talks about God. This is not a reading that adds new meanings to the first Testament, nor is it one that approves some things the first Testament says about God and rejects others, but one that enables us to see aspects of what is present in the way the first Testament talks about God that we might otherwise miss."[3]

God had ordained in His sovereignty that Judah receive the kingship, but God's move in Him required his cooperation as demonstrated in his repentance and return to his brothers for their reconciliation, for the sake of the kingdom. And so in light of who God is in Christ, we should appreciate the following principles concerning Judah and Tamar as they followed after the God of Abraham, Isaac, and Jacob on their pathway of kingship in the kingdom of God:

Judah

- Although Judah did wrong and fell, God sought after him for the kingship. In response, he confessed, recovered, and went back to his brothers. If today we hear His voice, we should not harden our hearts (Heb. 3:15). We need to learn from Judah and repent, that is we must make an about turn for the kingdom (Matt. 3:2, 4:17).

- Loving God's people, our brothers, is a key to blessing. After reverting to his brothers, Judah took care of Jacob (and also Benjamin) when his father was suffering under the conspiracy of his sons, to the extent that Judah sacrificed himself for their welfare. We need to do the same in our ministry of reconciliation in the church as the

---

3. J. Goldingay, *Key Questions about Biblical Interpretation*, 236.

kingdom of God (John 13:35; 15:12–13, 17; Heb. 10:24, 13:1).

- In doing the right things for God, we may have to "prevail over our brothers" to serve them in the way of reconciliation in the kingdom. In taking the lead for the reconciliation of Israel as a family, Judah prevailed over his brothers and was blessed with participation in God's promise to Abraham concerning the kingship. Such a service is exemplified in the apostle Paul in his laboring according to the grace of God. Our service to God in the kingdom for the sake of the believers in the churches should be patterned after Paul's ministry of reconciliation—laboring in the mold of the Lord's death and resurrection, in accordance with the grace that has been given to us that we may not run in vain (2 Cor. 5:18–19, Phil. 3:12–14, 2 Tim. 4:8).

Tamar

- No matter our situation, we need to have a heart for God. Although Tamar was a Gentile and her actions to regain the birthright was morally deplorable, there was a flip side to Tamar's unseemly scheming: she had a heart for the birthright, for righteousness, in that she desired to raise offspring to her deceased husband that his name might not be blotted out of Israel. Likewise we need to seek after the kingdom and its righteousness in service to others that they may be reconciled. Such a service to recover those who have fallen away is our birthright in the church of the firstborn (Matt. 5:6, 20; 6:33; Heb. 12:14–17; Rev. 22:11).

- Tamar's side tells us that we not only need to have a heart for the birthright, the things of God, we should even be anxious for it, trying our best to work it out according to the measure of grace given to us. We should emulate the apostle Paul— forgetting the things that are behind us and reaching forward toward the goal of God's high calling in Christ Jesus (Phil. 3:12–15, 2 Cor. 10:13, Matt. 11:12).

- But Perez and Zerah, her sons' side, balanced us in that we may strive, but ultimately it depends on God, on God's choice, not our efforts. This does not mean that we should do nothing. We should labor according to grace, but we must realize that it is not I but Christ and not I but the grace of God operating in us (Rom. 9:11, 1 Cor. 15:10) that enables us to accomplish what God in Christ had planned for us.

- In our endeavor in the kingdom, we should not use Tamar's unseemly acts as an excuse, and reason within ourselves that even if we do evil, good may come out of it. There was nothing in Tamar's heart that can be construed as evil. She had a heart for God and the people of God. Likewise, if we have a heart for the things of God and God's people, in time He will work things out to fulfill in us His purpose as seen in the examples of Tamar, and also Rahab, and Ruth in the genealogy that brought forth the King in His incarnation (Matt. 1:3, 5; Rom. 3:8, 8:28).

Richly and bountifully supplied for the kingdom The *energy* we see in Judah and Tamar; and as exemplified in Jesus and the apostles in their service in the kingdom is a testimony to the birthright we have inherited. Such a life and service as theirs is what the Lord Jesus alluded to when He told His disciples that He had food to eat of which they knew nothing, and that His "food" is to do the will of God who sent Him that He may accomplish God's work (John 4:32–34). Analogously, even as physical food gives to us physical energy, the operation of God within us as grace (the Spirit as the blessing of Abraham) supplies us with *divine energy*, the divine *energeia* that is none other than the power of resurrection of the God of Abraham, Isaac, and Jacob so we may will to do His will. The kingdom of God is constituted of such a life in resurrection. In resurrection Jesus is present to us as the operating Spirit for our experience of kingship in our service to others in the reconciliation. This experience conform us to the king's mold of coming not to be served but to be of service to others for the kingdom. For this very reason, the economy of grace is far more excellent than that of the law, for it not only demands but also supplies.

The will of God taken in this way becomes food to us as God's grace. But the operation of grace requires our obedience and cooperation. Yes, grace is our birthright, but we also need to will to do His will according to the God who operates in us both the willing and the working for His good pleasure (Phil. 2:13). That is why Paul wrote experientially that for him to know Christ was to know Him and the power of His resurrection and the fellowship of His sufferings, being conformed to Him in His death (Phil. 3:10). To be conformed to Christ's death is God's will for Paul. This is to be conformed to the *shape* of Christ's obedience unto death, and that the death of a cross. The only way for Paul to experience this energizing is for him to be molded to the pattern of Christ's death (vv. 5–11), that he may know the power of Christ's resurrection as the manifestation of life in his service.

The apostle's view was that to seek after Christ in this manner, according to God's energizing, is to pursue the prize for which God in Christ Jesus had called him upward (v. 14). The pathway of the cross is the track for our pursuing of Christ in the kingdom that we may reach the goal and attain the prize. In one sense, we have inherited the blessing of Abraham as grace; yet in another sense, we are to pursue a prize. Again the balanced viewpoint of God's ordination (our inheritance and birthright) is set against our responsibility in the kingdom to live, to pursue, and to labor according to His operation, which works in us in power. I say again, I believe in the assurance of salvation. But this is not about salvation in that sense;[4] it is about being supplied richly and bountifully with an entrance into the kingdom of our Lord

---

4. The negative points of the five warnings in Hebrews are related to some suffering of loss of reward. The reward of the kingdom or the loss of it is seen in many portions of Scripture. Only by acknowledging this can one rightly understand the many passages, such as Matt. 5:20; 7:21–23; 16:24–27; 19:3–30; 24:46–51; 25:11–13, 21, 23, 26–30; Luke 12:42–48; 19:17, 19, 22–27; Rom. 14:10, 12; 1 Cor. 3:8, 13–15; 4:5; 9:24–27; Rom. 14:10, 12; 1 Cor. 3:8, 13–15; 4:5; 9:24–27; 2 Cor. 5:10; 2 Tim. 4:7–8; Heb. 2:3; 4:1, 9, 11; 6:4–8; 10:26–31, 35–39; 12:16–17, 28–29; Rev. 2:7, 10–11, 17, 26–27; 3:4–5, 11–12, 20; 22:12. The witnesses of Scripture pointing to some form of reward or loss run from Matthew to Revelation and are just too numerous to explain away. God's salvation is

and Savior Jesus Christ (2 Pet. 1:11). To this end, the apostle Paul proclaimed at the end of his earthly sojourn that "henceforth there is laid up for me the crown of righteousness, which the Lord, the righteous judge, will award to me on that Day, and *not only to me* but also to *all who have loved* his appearing" (2 Tim. 4:8, emphasis added).

Without entering into a high realization of the God of resurrection, grace, and His operation in us for our kingdom life, pursuit, and service to Him; it is impossible to enter into the spirit of the word in the significance of the birthright, much less apply and experience what it means to seek it the way Tamar did in Genesis 38. As we have seen, the value that God and the community of the faithful attached to seeking the birthright in the canon is not just something that is peculiar only to the first Testament.

It is also laid out in Hebrews and in many other portions of the second Testament from Matthew to Revelation—in regard to the matter of reward. Yes, even for Christians, Scripture does speak about reward. We are saved and will not perish eternally, but from the perspective of kingship and the kingdom, there is a prize to be gained by diligently seeking and pursuing Christ according to the inward operation of the God of Abraham, Isaac, and Jacob. This is to work according to the indwelling operation of the Triune God in resurrection that we have inherited as the blessing of Abraham. It is grace operating in us to fulfill all that God meant for us to be

---

eternal (John 10:28–29), but whatever persuasion we hail from, sobriety and prudence dictate that it is only wise to acknowledge it is possible for genuine Christians to suffer some kind of loss in terms of reward. Therefore, we need to be watchful and vigilant concerning our life, living, and conduct in the church, the kingdom today.

in our walk with and service to Him, in the kingdom and for the kingdom.

In the same manner that the pre-incarnated Son recovered a fallen Judah in Genesis 38, Jesus in resurrection appeared to a backsliding Peter (because of his denial of Jesus), and recovered him by asking, "'Simon, son of John, do you love me more than these?' He said to him, 'Yes, Lord; you know that I love you.' He said to him, 'Feed my lambs.' He said to him a second time, 'Simon, son of John, do you love me?' He said to him, 'Yes, Lord; you know that I love you.' He said to him, 'Tend [shepherd] my sheep.' He said to him the third time, 'Simon, son of John, do you love me?' Peter was grieved because he said to him the third time, 'Do you love me?' and he said to him, 'Lord, you know everything; you know that I love you.' Jesus said to him, 'Feed my sheep'" (John 21:15–17). After charging him with the care of God's people, the Lord revealed to a recovered Peter the manner of his eventual martyrdom in the way of the kingdom (v. 18), and He said to him, "Follow me" (vv. 18–19). This is also a charge given to us, for He is the author of our salvation, who has been perfected through sufferings that He may be qualified to lead many sons into glory (Heb. 2:10).

Amen!

Conclusion This volume on Genesis 38 adheres to a ruled reading of Christian Scripture in a two-testament witness to Christ. In Part 1, we saw the need to demonstrate the pivotal position and organic unity of Genesis 38 from within the patriarchal narratives. Part 2 undertook this task from a historical, literary and structural perspective from the text of the story of the patriarchs—particularly that of the life of Jacob in God's move for the transmission of the birthright, the right of the firstborn. Part 3 presents the rule of faith, a ruled reading in accordance with the hypothesis of Christian Scripture in the order, connection, and arrangement of God's pre-incarnated and incarnated move in Christ across both Testaments.

In Part 4, we saw that the theme of the birthright is not only in the deep structure of the text of Genesis but also in the canonicity of *tota Scriptura*. Our reading of the two aspects of the birthright, God's sovereignty and man's responsibility, offers the opportunity for contextual theological reflection on present-day Christian heritage and responsibility with respect to the significance of law and grace in the context of the kingdom in the second Testament. Part 5 concludes with the experiential application of the God of Abraham, Isaac, and Jacob in the story of Judah and Tamar. As the God of resurrection in Christ, He is the indwelling Spirit in all those who believe. The Spirit that New Testament believers receive is the realization of Abraham's promise that even now operates in us as grace to supply us richly and bountifully. This is grace as our entrance into the eternal kingdom of our Savior, Jesus Christ.

We have thus attempted an interpretation of Genesis 38 within the normative canon of Scripture through the rule of faith. In so doing, we demonstrated the hypothesis that the unifying theme of kingship in the birthright is in the deep structure of Genesis and the whole Bible from multiple perspectives:

- We have seen the significance of birthright in the wider contextual pericope of Jacob within the patriarchal narratives in relation to God's promise to Abraham.

- We have seen that the historical background of the levirate custom is a direct allusion to a divine concern for the preservation of kingship as the birthright of the firstborn in relation to God's intention in creation.

- We have viewed God's sovereignty in His choosing of Judah for the kingship, from the perspective of Judah's story in Genesis—from his birth as the fourth son to his betrayal of Joseph, his backsliding, his recovery in Genesis 38, and his eventual inheritance of the kingship.

- We have portrayed the pivotal role of Genesis 38 from a time-extent perspective, highlighting the providence of God in recovering Judah who betrayed Joseph, and have presented Judah's role in the reconciliation of the house of Jacob as intertwined with his brother, Joseph.

- We also have seen the pivotal role of Genesis 38 from the perspective of the transmission of the birthright, concerning kingship, in the narrative of the patriarchs and as outlined in the life of Jacob, as well as the development of this theme in the entire Scripture from Genesis to Revelation.

- We have attempted a ruled reading of the story of Judah and Tamar from the move of God in the pre-incarnated

Christ in the first Testament to His move and operation as the God of resurrection (God of Abraham, Isaac, and Jacob) in the second Testament within believers as effective grace for their life, pursuit, and laboring in the ministry of reconciliation in the kingdom and for the kingdom today.

These are concrete verifications from the deep structure of the text and canon of Christian Scripture that such a proposed reading of Genesis 38 is both exegetical and Christological—as well as highly applicable to our experience today in the church as the kingdom of God. The hermeneutical tradition of the early church fathers is replete with similar reading traditions. They adhered to the rule of faith concerning the Son's move across both Testaments and accepted the significance of Genesis 38 in the canon, sometimes even against their natural sensibility.

Take for instance Cyril of Alexandria, Ephrem the Syrian, and Chrysostom:[5]

Cyril of Alexandria—"Although the text of the story does not seem very suitable, in Judah and Tamar the mystery of the incarnation of our Savior is described, which is the purpose of all scriptures,"

Ephrem the Syrian—"Although she (Tamar) was not an Israelite, she desired to receive the treasure hidden in the circumcised and prayed to God to move Judah to cooperate," and

---

5. T. C. Oden, gen. ed.; M. Sheridan, ed., *Ancient Christian Commentary on Scripture: Old Testament—Genesis Vol. II, 12–50* (Downers Grove, IL: IVP, 2002), 243.

Chrysostom—"Tamar's stratagem was by divine design, and her motives were good."

The readings of the church fathers have been labeled pre-critical by some moderns. But by and large, critical scholarships have veered from the authoritative interpretation of the first Testament as exemplified by Jesus, the apostles and the church fathers. However, God has not left Himself without witnesses, for I think recent scholarships' return to the rule of faith is a step forward in the right direction. There is much in the hypothesis of Scripture in its order and arrangement concerning the move of God in the Son that commends a reading of the first Testament that will lead adherents to Him who is life.

After all, this is the one thing that is necessary in our coming to the Scripture, for Jesus Himself had warned,

> "You search the Scriptures because you think that in them you have eternal life; and it is they that bear witness about me, yet you refuse to come to me that you may have life" (John 5:39–40).

So we do well to heed the examples of Jesus, the apostles and the church fathers. By way of last words, I would like to sum up the significance of the kingship portion of the birthright in relation to God as the God of Abraham, Isaac, and Jacob (the God of resurrection) in His move across both Testaments in these words:

> The dynamics of the birthright in the kingship and its transmission in the account of Jacob and his descendants is

rich. It captures the thought of participation in the covenant promise of Abraham as a special portion:[6] inheriting and experiencing an extra portion of the varied grace of the God of Abraham, Isaac, and Jacob (Exo. 3:6) in such a way that the God of resurrection (Heb. 11:17–19, Matt. 22:32, Mark 12:26, Luke 20:37) becomes our God and we become His people through His Triune saving operation in us.

This theme is first seen in God's dealings with the patriarchs, but it would span both Testaments in the work of the Son and will eventually culminate in our enjoyment of the kingdom along with Abraham, Isaac, and Jacob (Luke 13:28, Matt. 8:11). As such, it is the key to the interpretation of the patriarchal narratives; and, by extension, the story of Joseph, Judah, and Tamar takes on meaning within that. Such a reading—according to this imprint of God's Triune identity, as seen in His move and operation across both Testaments for the kingship—is representative of the character of Christian Scripture and is the significance of a two-Testament Bible that is the Christian's unique heritage.

---

6. Typified by the allotment of the double portion of the land in the Old Testament, an extra portion given to Joseph through his two sons—Ephraim and Manasseh. This does not mean that the other eleven tribes did not have a share, only that Joseph attained a special portion. In the New Testament, this is tied to the concept of reward or loss of it in relation to the kingdom. The reward of the kingdom should not be interpreted as wages for works, or works of the law, but rather a balanced teaching about grace, in that we are to cooperate with the operation of the Spirit who dwells within us. The apostle Paul spoke of his aspiration to attain the out-resurrection (Gk. *exanastasis*) from the dead, an extra portion he had not yet obtained when he wrote to the Phlippians; but He pursued the goal for the prize to which God in Christ Jesus had called him upward (Phil. 3:11, 14). In was not until 2 Timothy 4:8, nearing his martyrdom, that the apostle was confident he had attained this special portion. And concerning this pursuit, he charged that all who are full grown should have this mind, and if in anything we are otherwise minded, this also God will reveal to us (Phil. 3:15).

Appendices

A. Genesis 38 should be interpreted within the wider story of the life of Jacob

B. The story of Judah in Genesis: with Genesis 38 serving as a pivot for recovery

C. Outlining Genesis 38

D. Narrative Structure of God's Recovery from Generation to Generation

E. Unbroken Line of God's Recovery and Witness versus Man's Fall

F. Birthright—God's sovereignty/Man's responsibility

G. Time-Extent of Genesis 38

Appendix A

> # Genesis 38 should be interpreted within the wider story of the life of Jacob:
>
> **Life of Jacob**
> 1. Striving for blessing and being dealt with (25–31)
>   - A. **Striving for blessing (25–27)**
>   - B. **Forced to leave home (28)**
>   - C. Being dealt with in Haran (29–30)
>
>   *Esau to Jacob*
>   *Simeon and Levi cursed*
>
> 2. Being broken and depending on God for blessing (31–36)
>   - A. Redirected by God and fleeing Laban (31)
>   - B. Fearing Esau, being broken and blessed as Israel at Penuel (32)
>   - C. Welcomed by Esau/defilement of Dinah at Shechem (33–34)
>   - D. Reminded by God to return to Bethel/death of Rachel (35:1–20)
>   - E. **Defilement of Reuben/death of Isaac (35:21–29)** *Reuben lost it*
>   - F. Generation of Esau (36)
>
> 3. Maturing and becoming a blessing (37–50)
>   - A. Generation of Jacob: Joseph as favorite son (37)
>   - B. Judah as fallen and recovered son (38)
>   - C. Joseph as prisoner in Egypt (39–40)
>   - D. Joseph reigning in Egypt (41–42)
>   - E. Judah taking a lead in family reconciliation (43–44)
>   - F. Jacob's family reconciled in Egypt (45–50)
>   - Jacob blessing Pharoah (47:10)
>   - Jacob blessing Ephraim and Manasseh (48:13–20)
>   - Jacob blessing his sons (49:1–28)
>
>   *Where did the birthright go?*
>   *Who participated in its top blessings?*

The story of Judah in Genesis: **with Genesis 38 serving as a pivot for recovery**

Caption	Key Verses	Comment
Judah's birth and position	Gen. 29:35, 35:23	Judah is Jacob's fourth son through his wife Leah.
Role in Joseph's betrayal	Gen. 37:26–28	Judah proposed the sale of Joseph to the Ishmaelites.
Falling away	Gen. 38:1–11	Judah departed from his brothers, befriended an Adullamite and married a Canaanite.
Repentance and recovery	Gen. 38:12–20	Judah repented with the words, "She is more righteous than I ..." (v. 26).
Leading role in family reconciliation	Gen. 43:1–8, 44:1–34, 46:12, 28	During the famine Judah first pledged himself to Jacob as surety; and again to Joseph as replacement for Benjamin's release.
The approval of Judah in Jacob's prophesy concerning his sons	Gen. 49:8–12	"The scepter shall not depart from Judah, nor the ruler's staff from between his feet, until tribute comes to him; and to him shall be the obedience of the peoples" (v. 10).

Outlining Genesis 38

3. Life of Jacob: Maturing and becoming a blessing (37–50)
   A. Generation of Jacob: Joseph as favorite son (37)
   B. Judah as fallen and recovered son (38:1–30)
      1. Fall away after betraying Joseph (vv. 1–11)
         a. Departing from his brothers (v. 1)
         b. Marrying a Canaanite and fathering sons (vv. 2–5)
         c. Judah's sons and Tamar—violating Levirate
            marriage,
            putting participation in birthright at risk
            (vv. 6–11)

      2. Recover through Tamar's faithfulness (vv. 12–30)
         a. Tamar's unseemly scheme for participation in
            birthright (vv. 12–19)
         b. Tamar's vindication due to her faithfulness
            – Judah's confession(vv. 20–26)
         c. Participation in birthright gained: Pharez and Zerah
            (vv. 27–30)
   C. Joseph as prisoner in Egypt (39–40)
   D. Joseph reigning in Egypt(41–42)
   E. Judah taking a lead in family reconciliation (43–44)
   F. Jacob's family reconciled in Egypt: (45–50)
      - Jacob blessing Pharaoh (47:10)
      - Jacob blessing Ephraim and Manasseh (48:13–20)
      - Jacob blessing his sons (49:1–28)

Appendix D

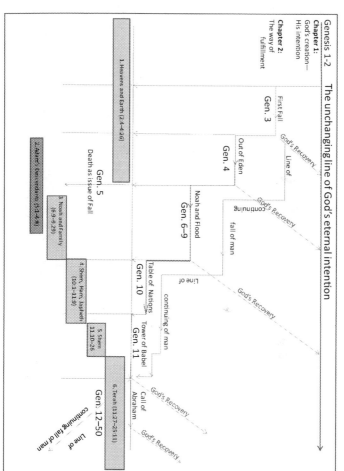

Narrative Structure of God's Recovery from Generation to Generation

Genesis 1-2   The unchanging line of God's eternal intention

Chapter 1:
God's creation—
His intention

Chapter 2:
The way of
fulfillment

First Fall
Gen. 3

Out of Eden
Gen. 4

God's Recovery   Line of

Gen. 5
Death as issue of Fall

Noah and Flood
Gen. 6–9

God's Recovery   continuing

fall of man

Table of Nations
Gen. 10

Line of

Tower of Babel
Gen. 11

continuing of man

God's Recovery

Call of
Abraham

Gen. 12–50

God's Recovery

God's Recovery

Line of   continuing fall of man

1. Heavens and Earth (1:1-4:26)

2. Adam's Descendants (5:1-6:8)

3. Noah and Family (6:9-9:29)

4. Shem, Ham, Japheth (10:1-11:9)

5. Shem 11:10-26

6. Terah (11:27-25:11)

Appendix E

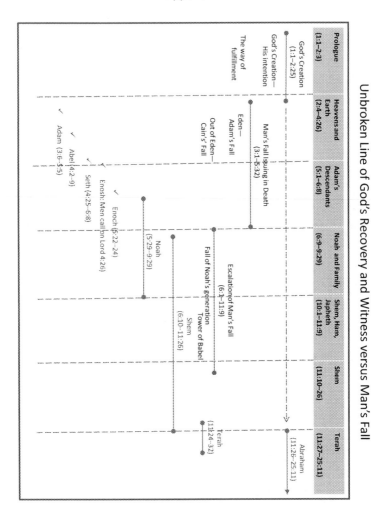

Unbroken Line of God's Recovery and Witness versus Man's Fall

| Prologue (1:1—2:3) | Heavens and Earth (2:4—4:26) | Adam's Descendants (5:1—6:8) | Noah and Family (6:9—9:29) | Shem, Ham, Japheth (10:1—11:9) | Shem (11:10—26) | Terah (11:27—25:11) |

God's Creation (1:1—2:25)

God's Creation— His intention

The way of fulfillment

Eden— Adam's Fall

Out of Eden— Cain's Fall

Man's Fall Issuing in Death (3:1—5:32)

Adam (3:6—5:5)

Abel (4:2—9)

Seth (4:25—5:8)

Enosh: Men call on Lord 4:26)

Enoch (5:22—24)

Noah (5:29—9:29)

Escalation of Man's Fall (6:1—11:9)

Fall of Noah's generation

Tower of Babel

Shem (6:10—11:26)

Terah (11:24—32)

Abraham (11:26—25:11)

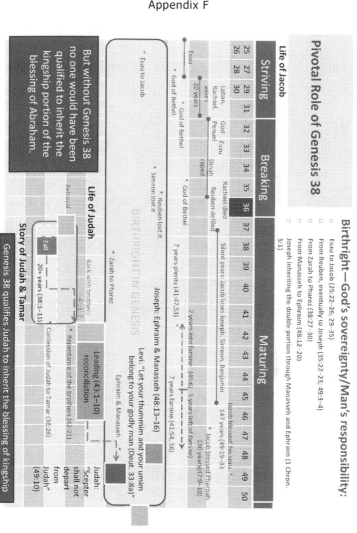

Pivotal Role of Genesis 38

Birthright—God's sovereignty/Man's responsibility:

○ Esau to Jacob (25:22–26; 29–35)
○ From Reuben, eventually to Joseph (35:22–23; 49:3–4)
○ From Zarah to Pharez (38:27–30)
○ From Manasseh to Ephraim (48:12–20)
○ Joseph inheriting the double portion through Manasseh and Ephraim (1 Chron. 5:1)

Life of Jacob

Striving						Breaking					Maturing														
25	26	27	28	29	30	31	32	33	34	35	36	37	38	39	40	41	42	43	44	45	46	47	48	49	50

* Esau to Jacob

* God of Bethel

Esau

Laban, Rachael, wives 20 years

God Penuel Esau

Dinah raped

Rachael died Reuben defiled

* God of Bethel

* Reuben lost it

* Simeon lost it

* God of Bethel

7 years plenty (41:47,53)

Silent years: Jacob loses Joseph, Simeon, Benjamin

2 years into famine (45:6), 5 years left of famine)

7 years famine (41:54, 56)

147 years, Jacob blessed his sons

* Jacob blessed Pharaoh 130 years (47:9-10)

* Jacob blessed his sons (49:19–33)

Life of Judah

Bethulah

Fall

20+ years (38:1–11)

4:1–7

* Zarah to Pharez

Back with brothers

Zarah to Pharez

* Repentance of the brothers (42:21)

Confession of Judah to Tamar (38:26)

Joseph: Ephraim & Manasseh (48:13–16)

Levi: "Let your thummim and your umim belong to your godly man (Deut. 33:8a)"

Ephraim & Manasseh

Leading (43:1–10) reconciliation

Ephraim & Manasseh

Judah: "Scepter shall not depart from Judah" (49:10)

BIRTHRIGHT IN GENESIS

Story of Judah & Tamar

Genesis 38 qualifies Judah to inherit the blessing of kingship

But without Genesis 38 no one would have been qualified to inherit the kingship portion of the blessing of Abraham.

Pivotal Role of Genesis 38

Time-extent of Genesis 38—"And it came about at that time ..." (v. 1):
- Probable time span for Gen. 38: 1–11, 20+ years; vv.12-30, less than 1 year
- During these years:
  - Joseph was being prepared to rule in Egypt
  - Judah was being prepared to assume leadership role among his brothers

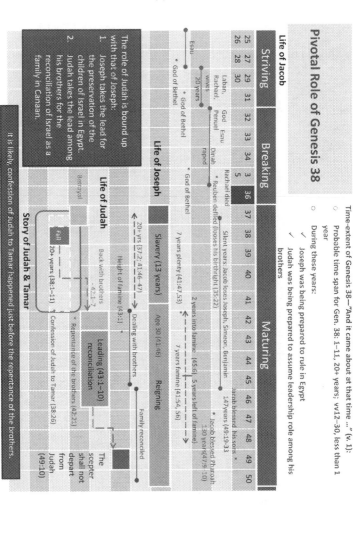

The role of Judah is bound up with that of Joseph:
1. Joseph takes the lead for the preservation of the children of Israel in Egypt.
2. Judah takes the lead among his brothers for the reconciliation of Israel as a family in Canaan.

it is likely, confession of Judah to Tamar happened just before the repentance of the brothers.

BIBLIOGRAPHY

Childs, B. S. *Introduction to the Old Testament as Scripture*. Philadelphia: Fortress Press, 1979.

———. *Old Testament Theology in Canonical Context*. Philadelphia: Fortress Press, 1986.

Goldin, J. *The Youngest Son or where Does Genesis 38 Belong*. JBL 96, 1977.

Goldingay, J. *Key Questions about Biblical Interpretation: Old Testament Answers*. Grand Rapids, MI: Baker Academic, 2011.

Green, J. B. *Practicing Theological Interpretation: Engaging Biblical Texts for Faith and Formation*. Grand Rapids: Baker Academics, 2011.

Greidanus, S. *Preaching Christ from Genesis: Foundations for Expository Sermons*. Grand Rapids: Eerdmans, 2007.

Harris, R. L., G. L. Archer Jr., and B. K. Waltke. *Theological Wordbook of the Old Testament: Vol. I, Aleph to Mem*. Chicago: Moody Press, 1980.

Kaiser, W. C. *Mission in the Old Testament: Israel as a Light to the Nations*. Grand Rapids: Baker, 2000.

Kaiser Jr., W. C. "The Spirit Baptism in the Holy Spirit as the Promise of the Father: A Reformed Perspective" in *Perspectives on Spirit Baptism*, edited by C. O. Brand. Nashville: B&H, 2004.

Leupold, H. C. *Genesis II*. Grand Rapids: Baker, 1942.

Merrill, E. H., ed. *The Bible Knowledge Key Word Study: Genesis to Deuteronomy*. Colorado Springs: Cook, 2003.

Oden, T. C., gen. ed., and M. Sheridan, ed. *Ancient Christian Commentary on Scripture: Old Testament—Genesis Vol. II, 12–50*. Downers Grove, IL: IVP, 2002.

Richards, L. O. *New International Encyclopedia of Bible Words: Based on the NIV and NASB*. Grand Rapids: Zondervan, 1991.

Ross, A. P. *Creation and Blessing: A Guide to the Study of Genesis*. Grand Rapids: Baker, 1998.

Sailhamer, J. H. *The Pentateuch as Narrative*. Grand Rapids: Zondervan, 1992.

Seitz, C. R. *The Character of Christian Scripture: The Significance of a Two-Testament Bible*. Grand Rapids: Baker Academics, 2011.

Sidney, G. *Preaching Christ from Genesis: Foundations for Expository Sermons*. Grand Rapids: Eerdmans, 2007.

Tragelles, S. P., trans. *Gesenius' Hebrew-Chaldee Lexicon of the Old Testament: Numerically Coded to Strong's Exhaustive Concordance*. Grand Rapids: Baker, 1979.

Treier, D. J. *Introducing Theological Interpretation of Scripture: Recovering a Christian Perspective*. Grand Rapids: Baker Academics, 2008.

Von Rad, G. *Genesis: A Commentary by Gerhard Von Rad*. 2nd ed. Philadelphia: The Westminster Press, 1972.

Waltke, B. K., with Cathi J. Fredricks. *Genesis: A Commentary*. Grand Rapids: Zondervan, 2001.

Walton, J. H., V. H. Matthews, and M. W. Chavalas. *The IVP Background Commentary: Old Testament*. Downers Grove: IVP, 2000.

Watchman, N. *The Collected Works of Watchman Nee: The God of Abraham, Isaac, and Jacob*, set two, vol. 35. Anaheim: LSM, 1993.

Westermann, C. *Genesis 37–50: A Continental Commentary*. Minneapolis: Fortress, 2002.

Wilson, J. M. "Birthright" in *The International Standard Bible Encyclopedia*, edited by James Orr. Peabody, MA: Hendrikson, 1994.

SCRIPTURE INDEX

About the Author

JOSEPH Ng Bak Soon has served in full time Christian ministry for many years. He has been involved in international Christian outreach programs, church planting, conferences, seminars, training of Christian workers and bible translation. He is an avid student of Scripture and a concerned Christian who has written numerous papers on contemporary subjects of interest at graduate seminary level.

Joseph is also a business and technology strategist with advanced graduate degrees relevant to his profession. His professional area of specialization is business/technology strategies for the financial sector with a focus on effective execution and implementation.

In his spare time, he runs—consistently averaging sixty kilometers per week for many years. That is more than three thousand kilometers of recreational running every single year. This may not be much when stacked up against the performance of professional runners. Still, at the rate he is going, he hopes to pile up enough mileage to circumnavigate the globe every fifteen years or so.

Joseph wishes to engage the public on all areas of Christian life, living, and experience through a series of online as well as offline writing projects.

Printed in the United States
By Bookmasters